AF589602

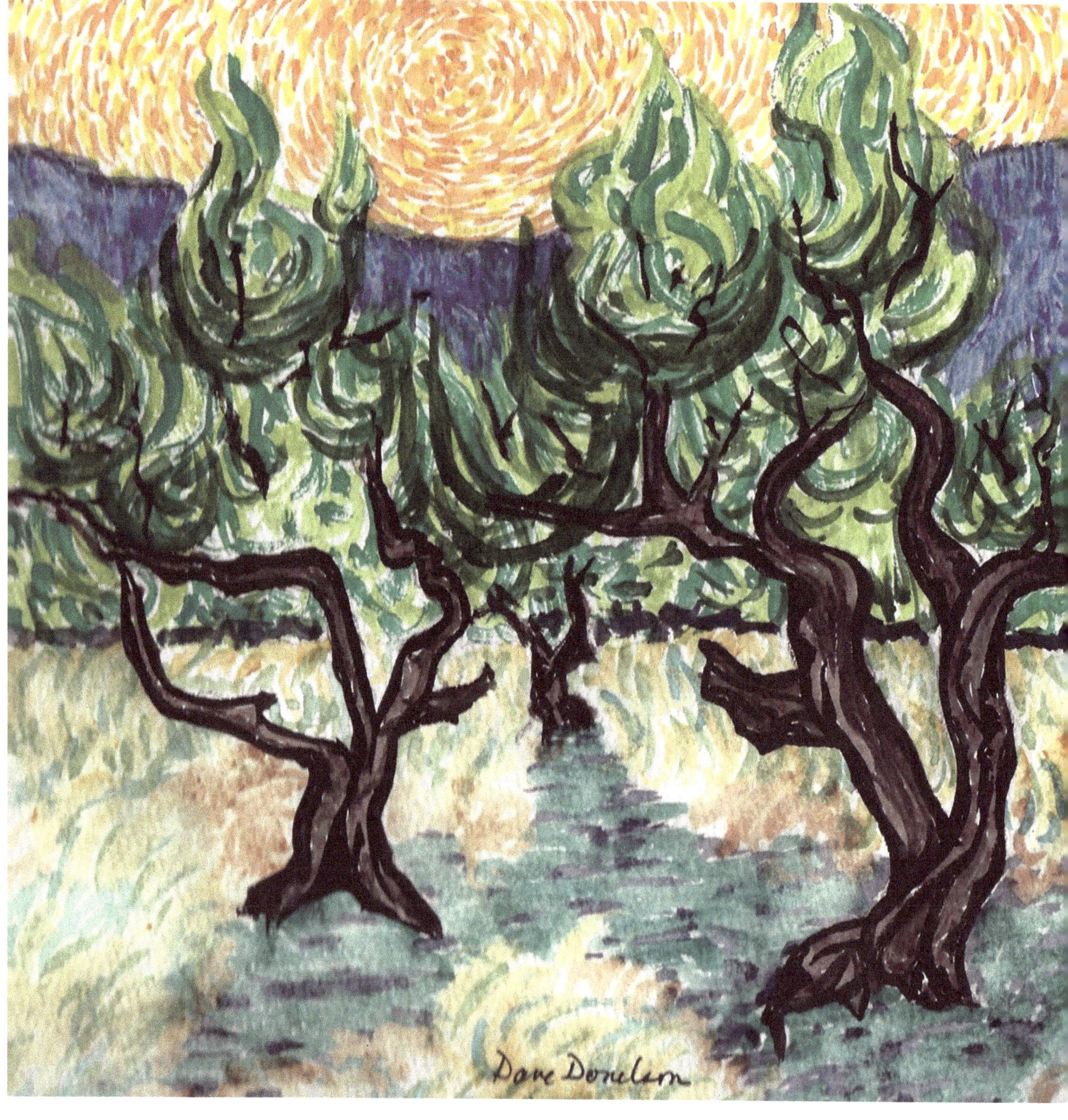
Dave Donelson

Provence Reflections

Dave Donelson

DSDA, Inc.

Provence Reflections

Copyright © 2024 by Dave Donelson.

All Rights Reserved. Published and printed in the United States of America by Donelson SDA, Inc. No part of this book may be reproduced, copied or used in any form or manner whatsoever without written permission, except in the case of brief quotations in reviews and critical articles.

For information, contact Donelson SDA, Inc.

44 Park Lane, West Harrison, NY 10604

FIRST EDITION

Acknowledgments

We extend our thanks to Backroads, the excellent travel company

that orchestrated our visit to Provence.

Special thanks go to Laura Opitz,

the highly capable and ever-cheerful leader of the trip.

Disclaimer : This is a work of imagination. Any depictions of real persons, entities, or companies is purely dependent on the author/photographer's candid access to them in public spaces. Real brand names, company names, names of public personalities or real people may be employed for credibility because they are part of our culture and everyday lives. Regardless of context, their use is meant neither as endorsement nor criticism: such images and names are used fictitiously without intent to describe their actual conduct or value. Many other names, products or brands are inventions of the author's imagination. Donelson SDA, Inc. and its directors, employees, distributors, retailers, wholesalers and assigns disclaim any liability or responsibility for the author's statements, words, ideas, criticisms or observations. Donelson SDA, Inc., assumes no responsibility for errors, inaccuracies, or omissions.

For Nora,
my treasured companion
on life's adventures

Reflections

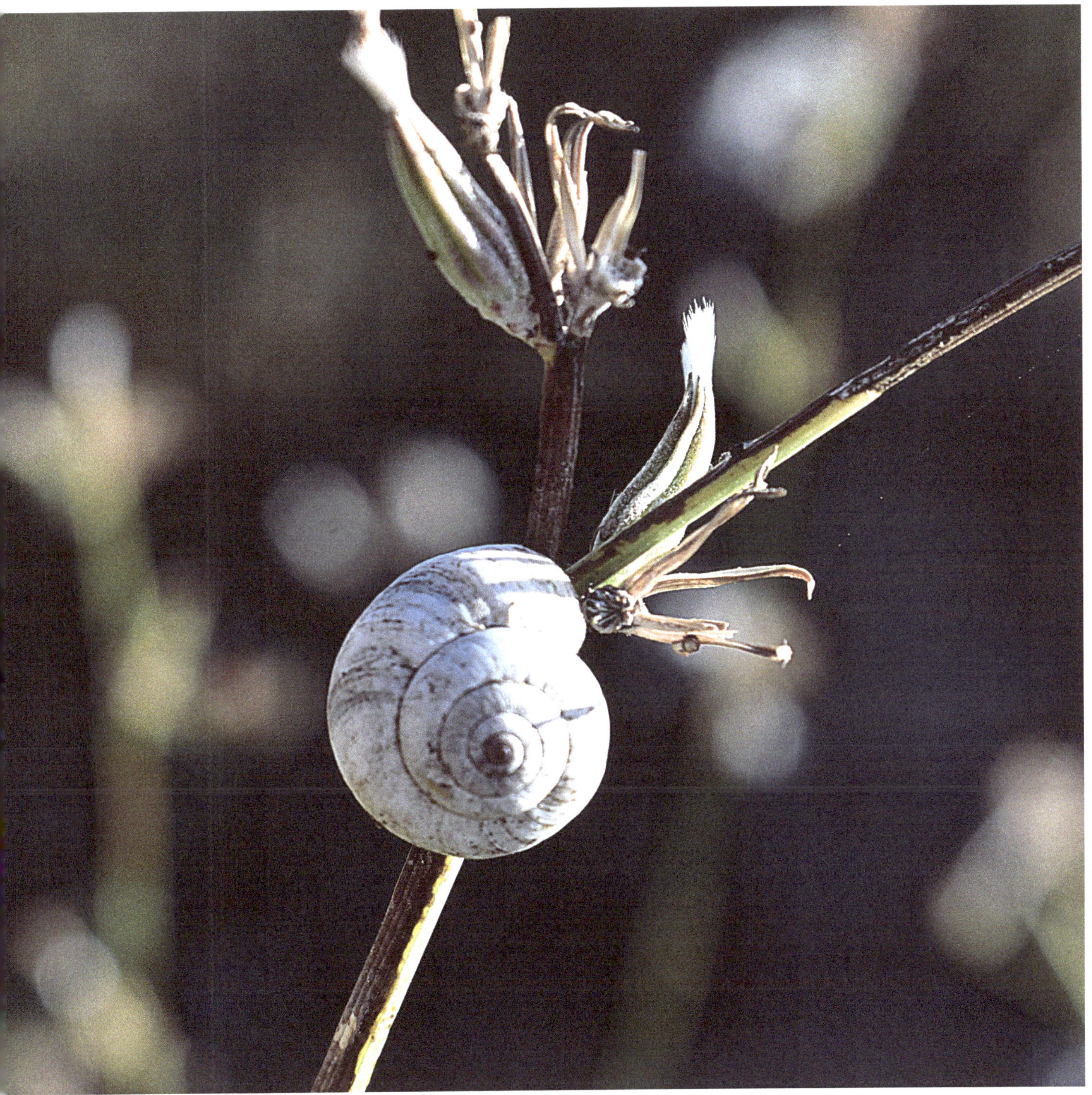

Reflections

If I hadn't stopped to retie my boot, I never would have noticed the tiny white snails clustered on the stubble of the wheat field along the Grande Randonnee Trail we hiked in Provence. From a few feet away, they looked like a string of bubbles on the stems of the recently harvested grain. Leaning closer, I realized they had whorled shells the size of a fingernail and, looking more closely still, I saw miniscule eyes mounted on hair-thin tentacles growing from the top of their heads.

Questions arose the longer I looked. What did they eat? The farmer's wheat? The grapes in the vineyard on the other side of the road? I should look for them on the vines, I thought. Could they be eaten themselves, perhaps steamed and picked from their shells and served with garlic butter on a crust of bread made from the farmer's wheat? They were small creatures with the power to halt, for me, the passage of time.

Art can do the same thing. An Auguste Chabaud landscape or one of Van Gogh's wheatfield paintings give me pause. I stop to think about not just what they depict, but to consider what the artist intended to portray. The hurly-burly lives we lead seldom leave much time for such reflection, which is a shame because pausing to quietly examine the experiences we've had, the world we've seen, the things we've learned along the way, is very much how we make those lives worthwhile. Life rewards us not only when we live it, but even more richly when we hold it still and look at it closely as I did the snails. When we ask it questions and listen carefully to its answers. When we reflect.

As the title says, this book is about reflections. It is not a guidebook, but rather a collection of verbal and visual thoughts inspired by a brief vacation in Provence. It contains much about art and artists, because many, many artists came to Provence. Matisse, Monet, Renoir, Chagall, Gaugin, and, of course, Van Gogh. Picasso visited often and one of his long-suffering lovers, Dora Maar, an artist herself, lived there much of her life. Cezanne was born in Provence and returned again and again.

The question is why? They didn't come for the galleries or the urban nightlife, for salons and socialization. Did they come for the food? Perhaps, although not for the wine which is typically rather mediocre. Was it the air, fresh and briskly breezed? Or the famous sunlight, remarkably intense and pure? That's a widely-held belief, one hard to deny since pure light inspires brilliant colors, crisp shadows, and clarity of vision.

I think they came to simplify their lives in a place without the hustle and traffic of Paris. Where the urban circus didn't suck them into its three rings of competition, comparison, and professional jealousy. Provence was—and still is, despite the tourists—a place with few distractions other than quaint restaurants on winding, picturesque streets. The artists then, as now, can be one with their work and not be looking over their shoulders in dread of a judgmental eye. They have time to reflect.

I did a great deal of reflecting while in Provence and even more when we returned as I began painting and writing about the trip. I've put those reflections into this book in several forms. Some are imagined pieces written in the voices of artists who were powerfully influenced by their lives in Provence. You might notice that I often use the artists' own words in those pieces. These I sometimes altered to fit the context of the piece, although I tried to not change the meanings of what they said and wrote. You will also find my versions of a couple of fables and a little history of the region. Most of the book, though, consists of photographs and sketches from the trip and paintings done after. When appropriate, I include a black and white reference photo that inspired a given painting.

This book, in other words, expresses a few moments of reflections on art, life, and Provence.

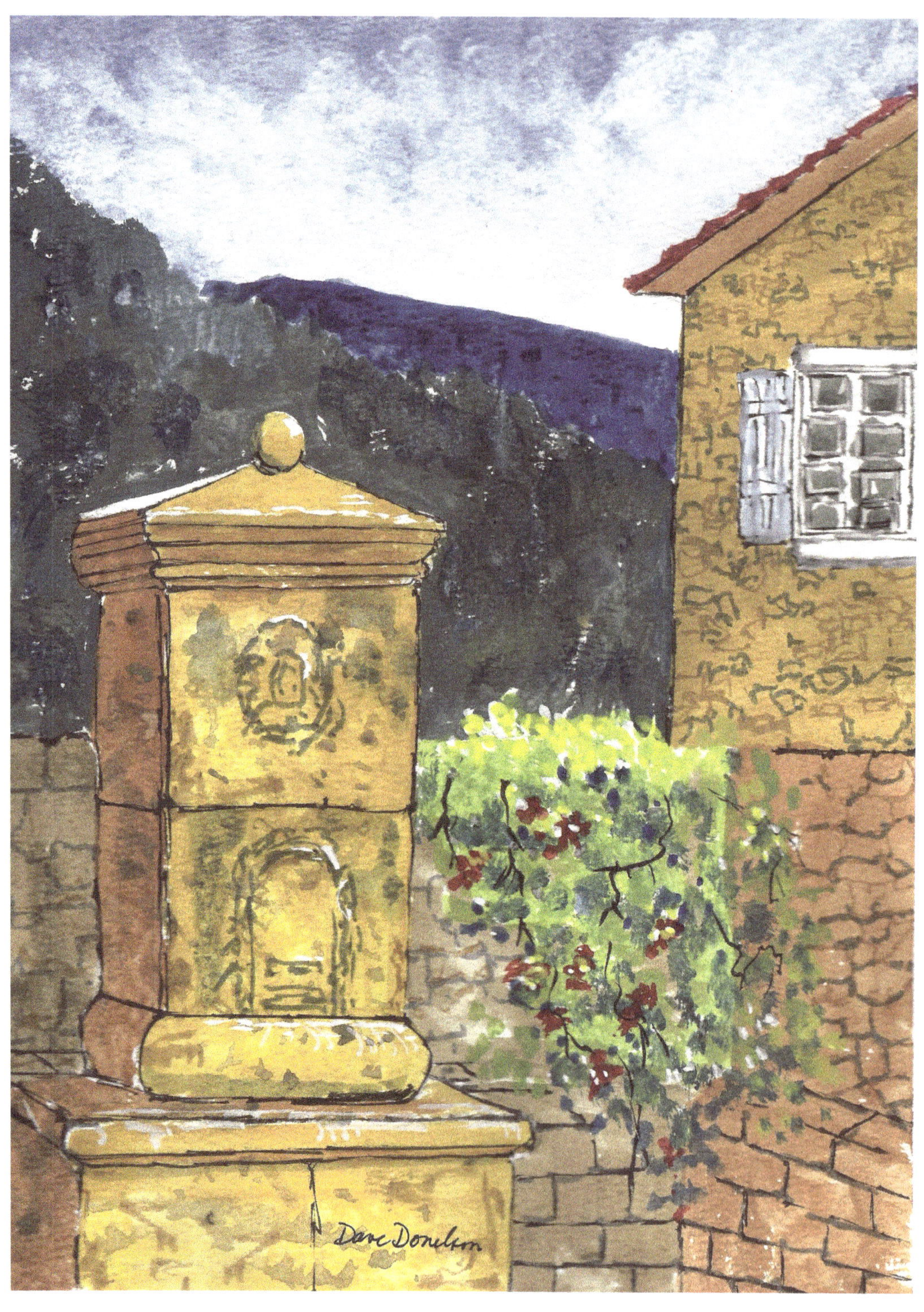
Dave Donelson

Chapter One
Native Son

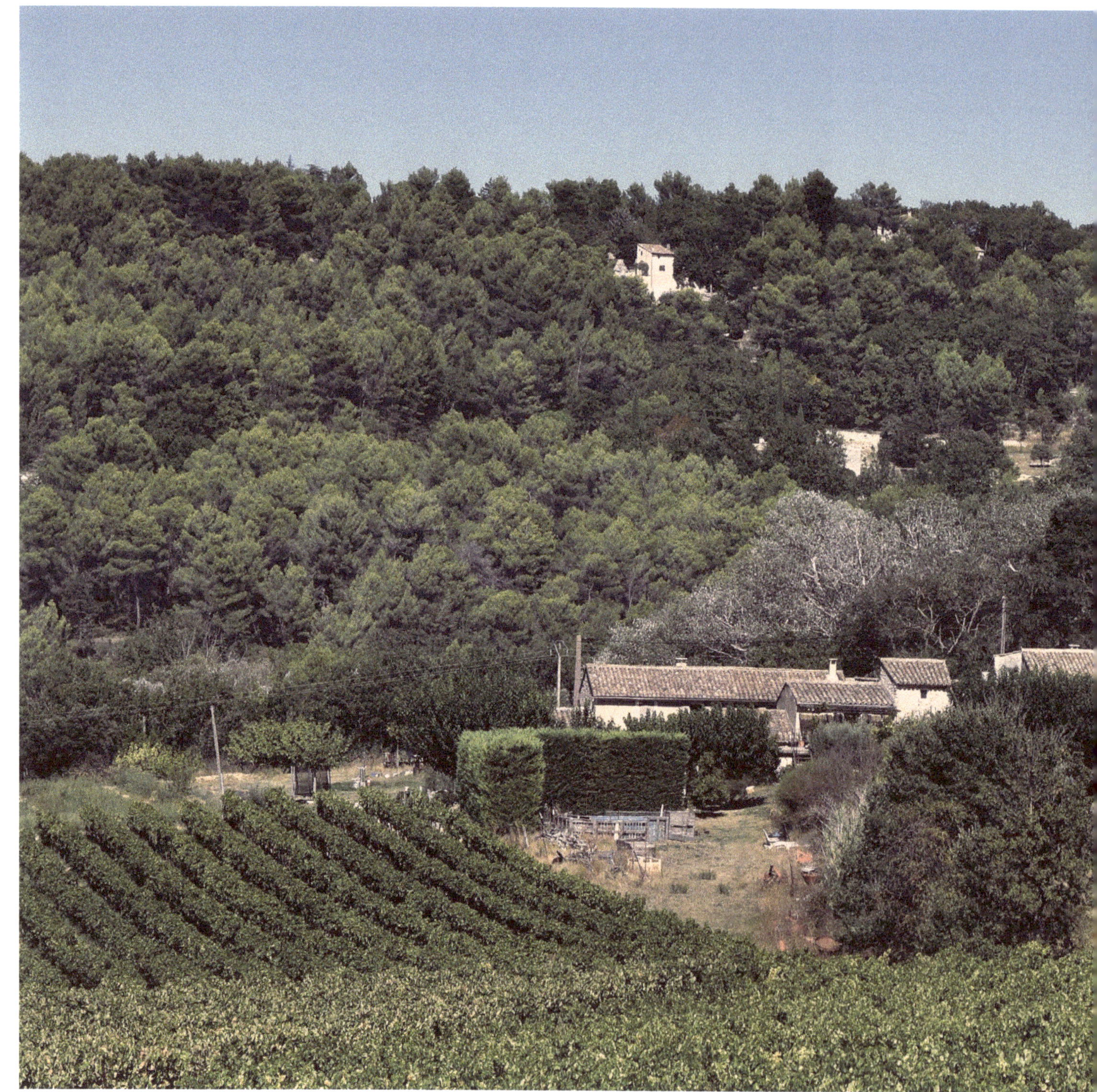

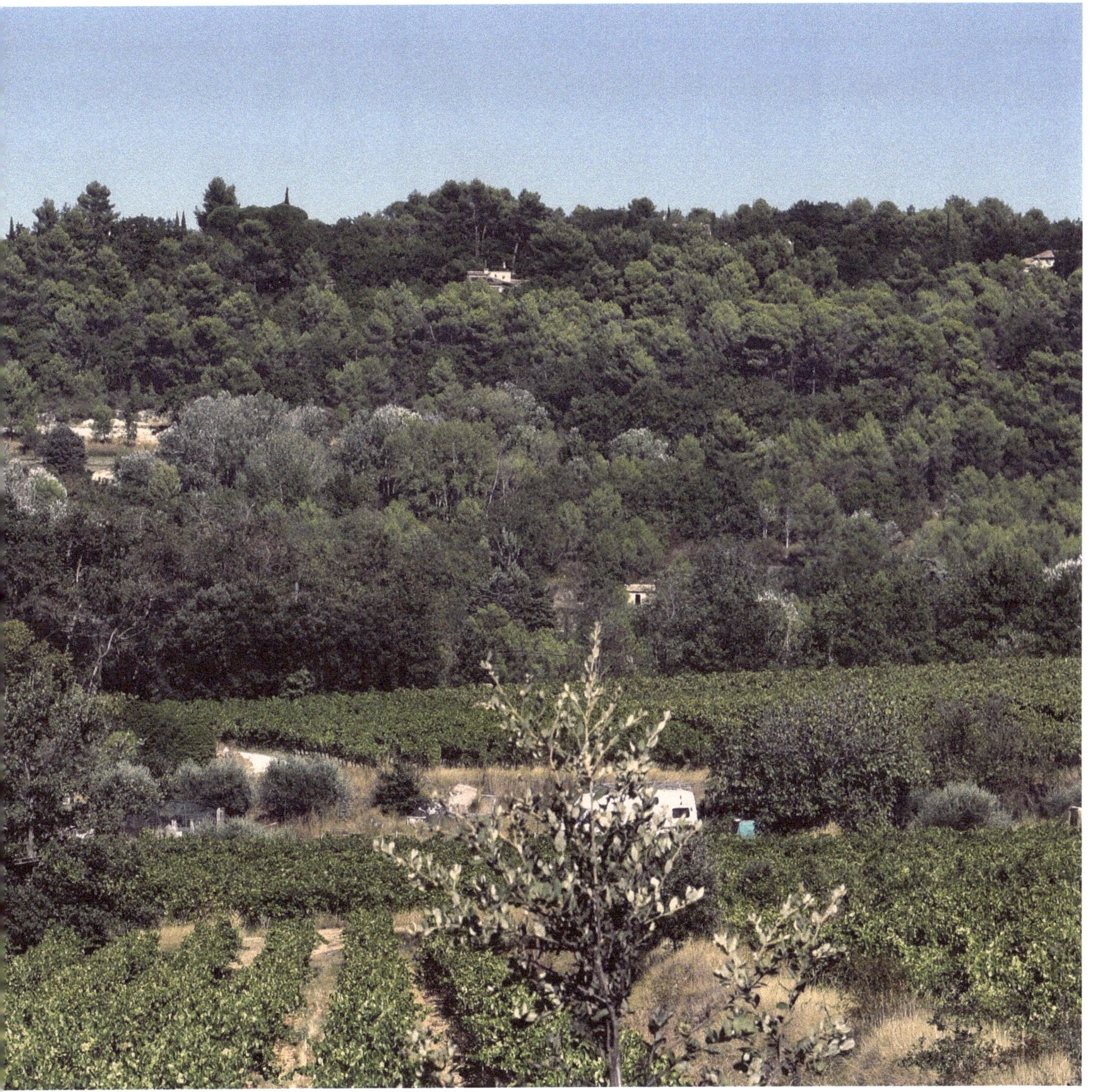

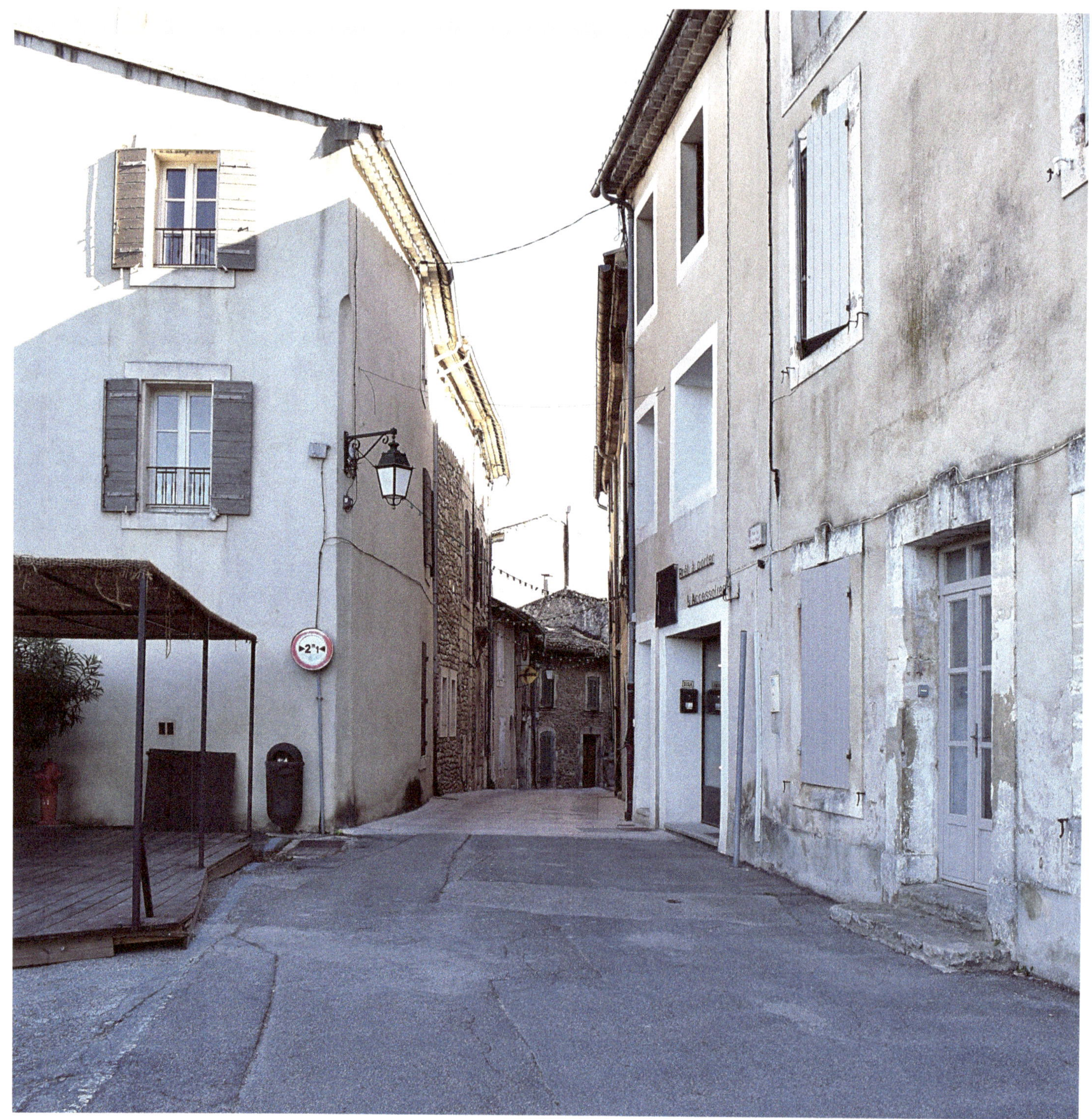
Prêt à porter
& Accessoires

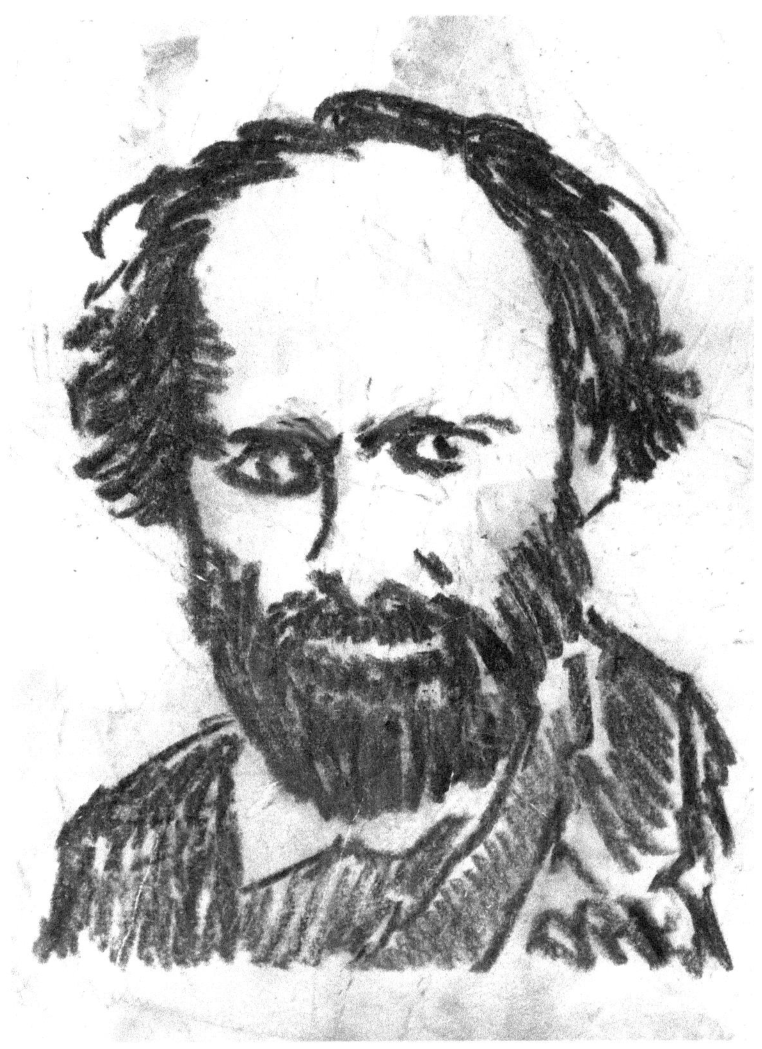

Paul Cezanne's Letter to Emile Zola

My dear, dear Emile,

The news of your passing into the next world saddens me beyond measure. Not only have I lost the only man who ever understood me, I have lost my most true defender. And I miss your protection now more than ever.

The ignorant critics berate me and my art as they have from the beginning when I first tried to gain recognition from the Academy and then from the Salon. They mock me even over your grave, calling the paintings by me that you had collected "Love for the ugly," revealing not only their evil, vitriolic natures but their blind ignorance. They do not understand that painting from nature does not mean copying the object, it means realizing its sensations. They can clearly never recognize that something other than reality is what I endeavor to discover and reveal.

But I miss your protection from the petty bourgeoise of Aix as well. Many of them, I am sure, are the same bullies from whom I guarded you in those glorious years of our youth in this benighted village. They have begun sending me threatening letters and even leaving copies of disparaging reviews on my doormat with notes demanding that I leave the town they claim I dishonor. Were it not that I am deeply in love with the landscape of my country, I should not be here.

You know what I mean about the beauty of the land of our childhood. There's a sadness in Provence which no one has expressed. I'd like to combine melancholy and sunshine, put reason in the grass and tears in the sky. I am old enough now to know how to read what I see to better understand its essential colors and forms. These must be the dominant elements of my compositions. I will not bow to the stiff rules of perspective dictated by the Academy.

Were you here, you would comprehend immediately what I am doing now. You watched my work evolve from strangled efforts to depict reality to bold application of paint to reveal the absolute meaning of the subject. It is the colored surfaces where the soul trembles, where the prismatic warmth radiates in the sunlight. I now design my surfaces with the shades on my palette so they are clearly visible. Everything must play together and yet create contrasts.

At this late time in my life, I now paint mostly two subjects, the Mont Sainte Victoire I can see from my studio, and groups of bathers frolicking nude in nature as once we did. The more I paint, the more I come to believe that art is a harmony parallel to nature.

If you were alive to see the work I paint today, you would quickly grasp how I treat nature according to cylinder, sphere, and cone, and put the whole in perspective so that each side of an object, each surface, leads to a central point. It's all about volume. Others are grasping this idea and carrying it to extremes in paintings that draw praise that mine never did. Oh, Emile, if only you were still on this earth to be my champion!

For I desperately need someone to speak for me. All of the painter's intentions must be silent. He should silence his internal voices of prejudice. Forget! Forget! Create silence and be a perfect echo of the elemental essence of the subject.

Do you understand? The landscape is reflected in me. I climb to the roofs of the world. A tender excitement seizes me and from its roots rises the juice, the color. In order to paint that, craft must be used, but a humble craft that obeys and transmits unconsciously.

Some may think such excitement leads to a hurried, slap-dash process, but nothing could be further from the truth. I struggle to realize my visions on the canvas. Were you to watch me, you would marvel that I may ponder a single brush stroke for hours before touching the brush to the paint. The work does not spring full-formed in minutes. All too often, even after days devoted to a piece, I discover it fails to achieve my vision and must be destroyed. Such is the discipline required of an artist, a discipline you know very well.

Unfortunately, few in this community understand the way an artist works or why. From this ignorance is born ridicule and prejudice. I know I am not a hale-fellow-well-met. I cannot live solely to meet the expectations of these people. It would be against my nature and would destroy me. I don't understand the world and the world doesn't understand me, so I withdraw from the world.

I will never withdraw from the memory of you, dear Emile. I do not know what awaits when I pass from his earth as you did, but my only hope is that we will be together once again.

Always and forever yours,

Paul

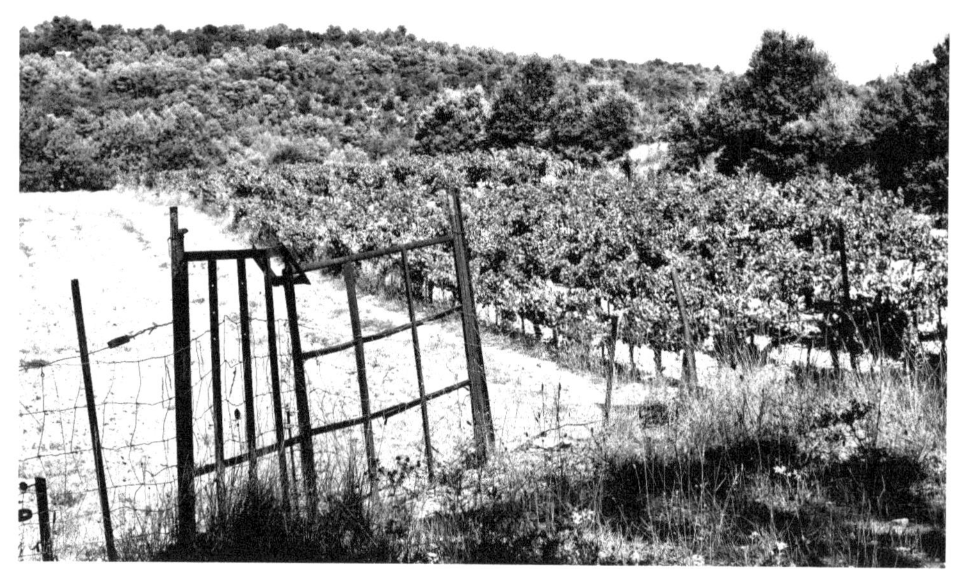

The artist works alone
Amidst a crowd of critics
Who can never know
What he sees or how it feels
To open a grasping gate

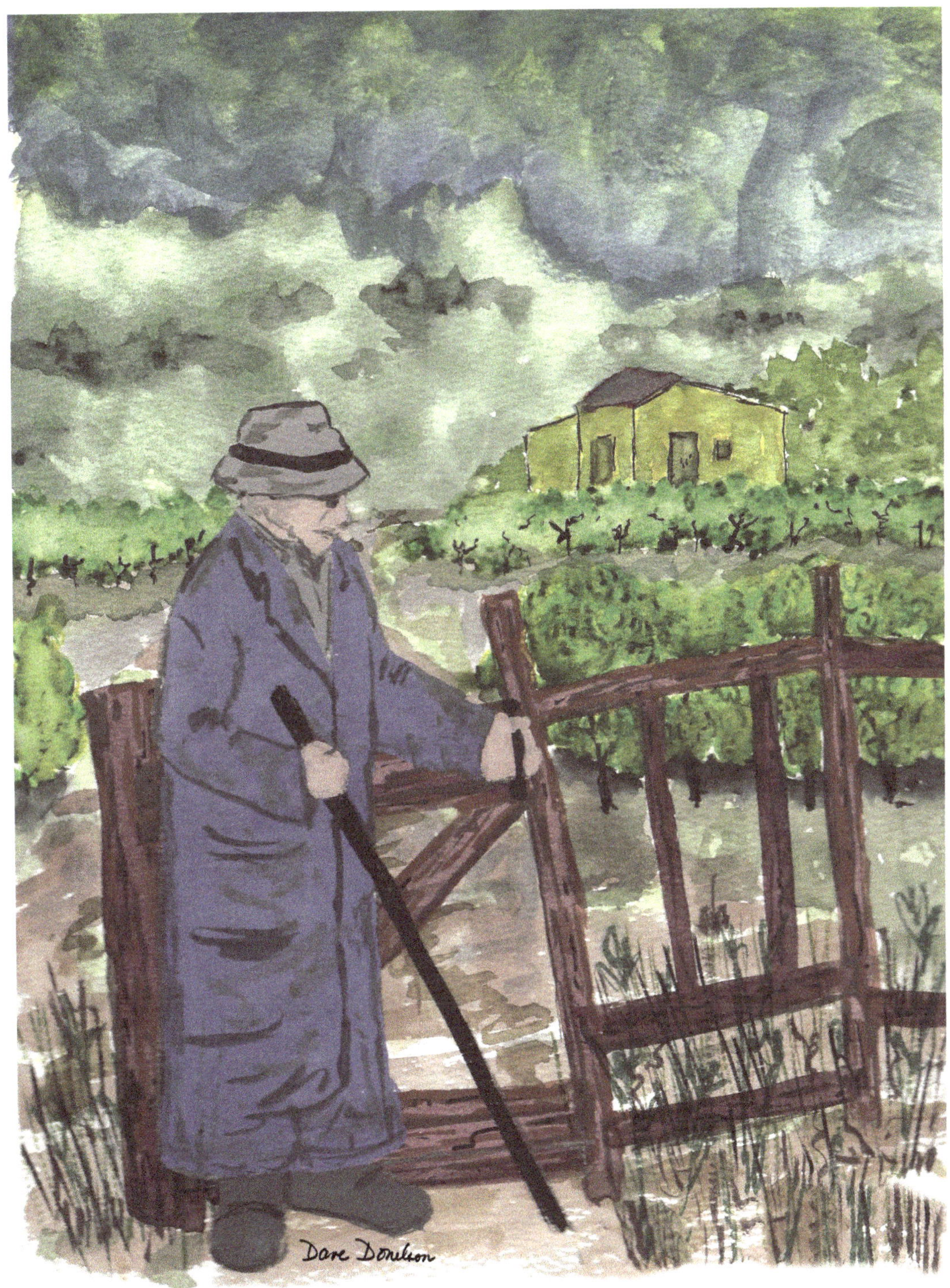
Dave Donelson

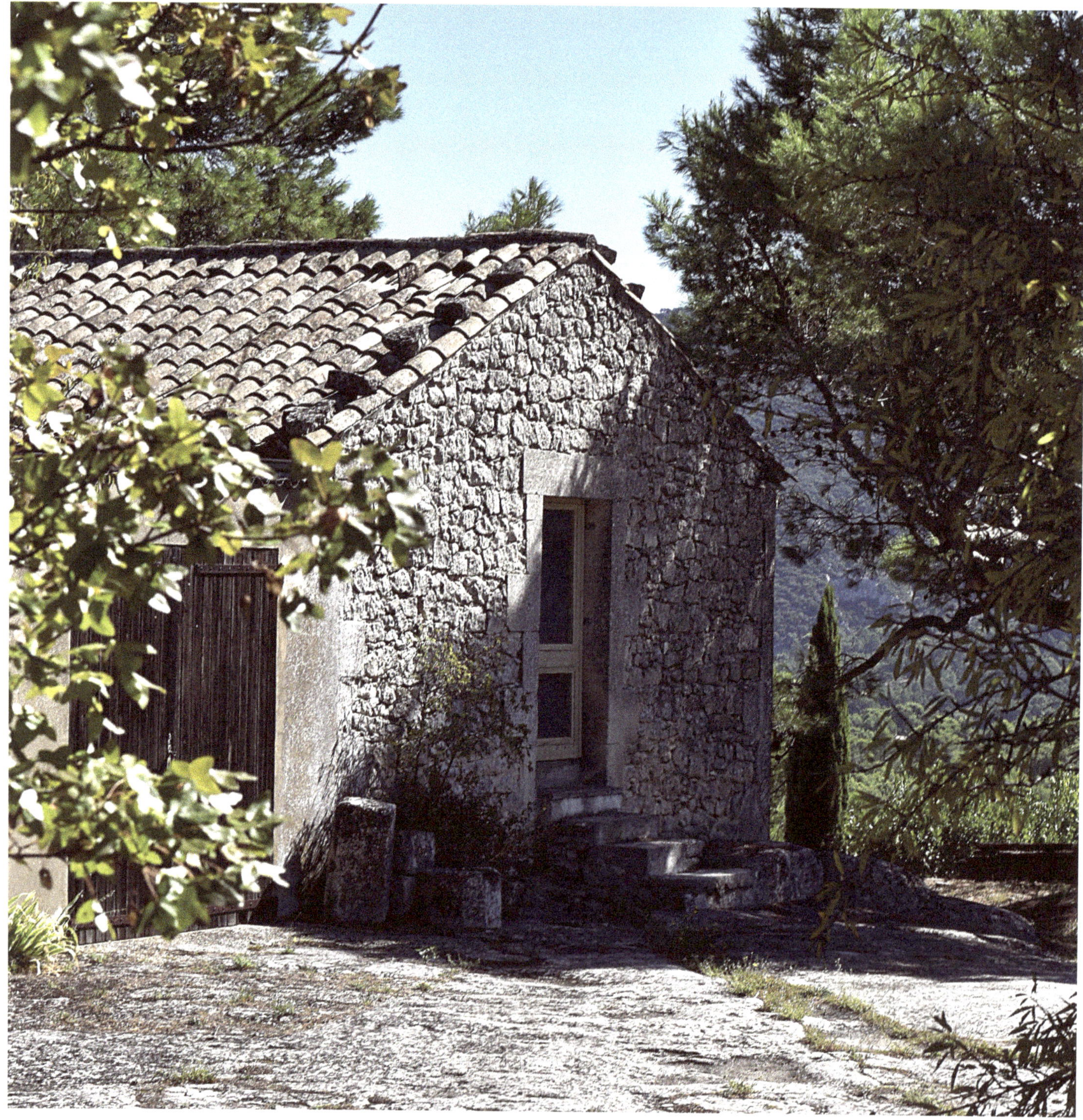

The stone house sits heavy, solid on the earth from which it came.

Its walls grew stone by stone, dug, cut, fitted, mortared, stacked to the roof line.

The mason with knowing hands chose each one by eye to snuggle the next.

His plumbline kept the wall straight to the earth while his level squared it to the horizon.

The farmer will leave the stone house to his children and they to theirs.

And they to theirs.

Those called others
Live in Provence
As elsewhere,
Black in a white sea,
Seeking refuge, sanctuary,
Always different, apart

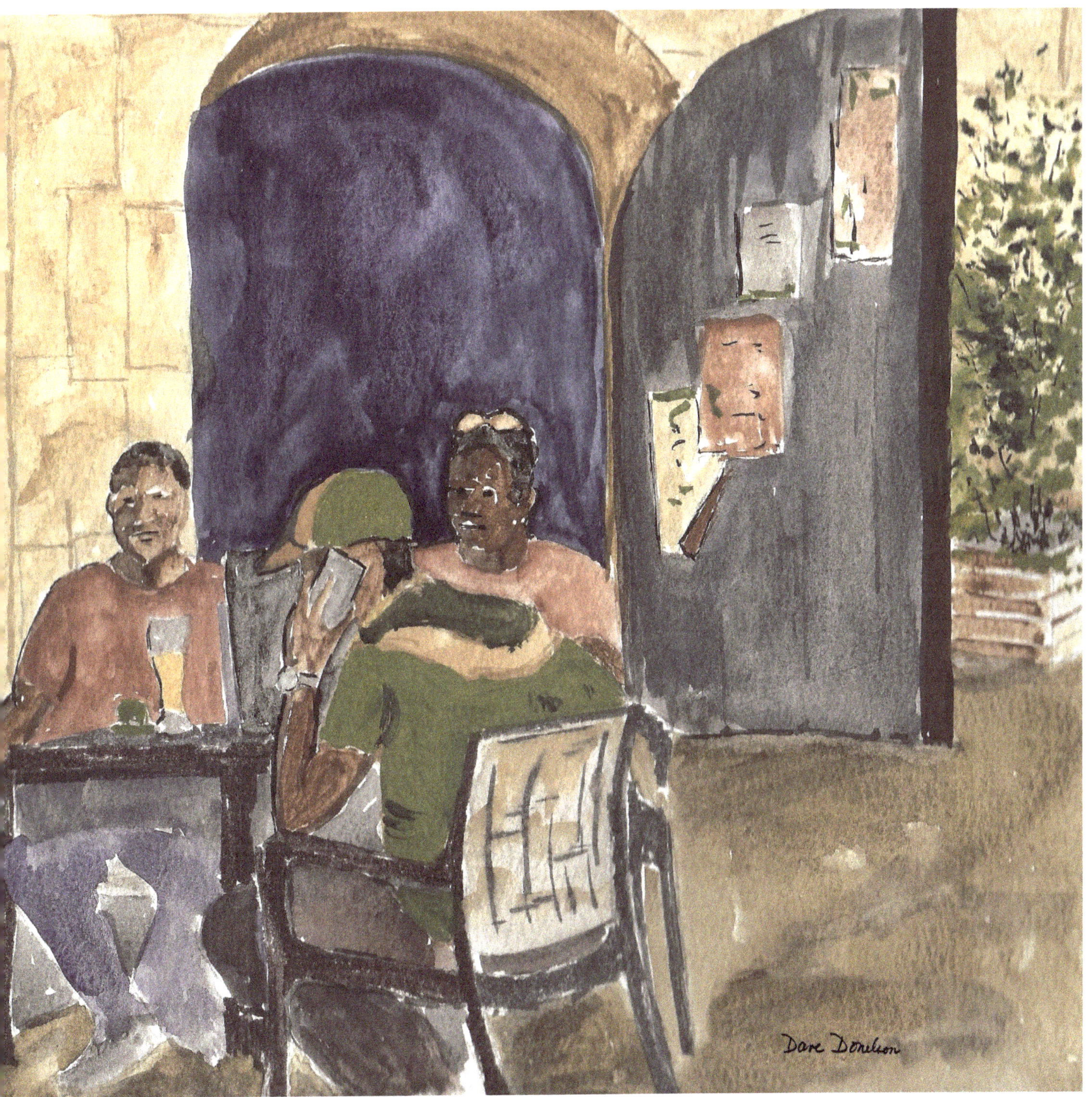

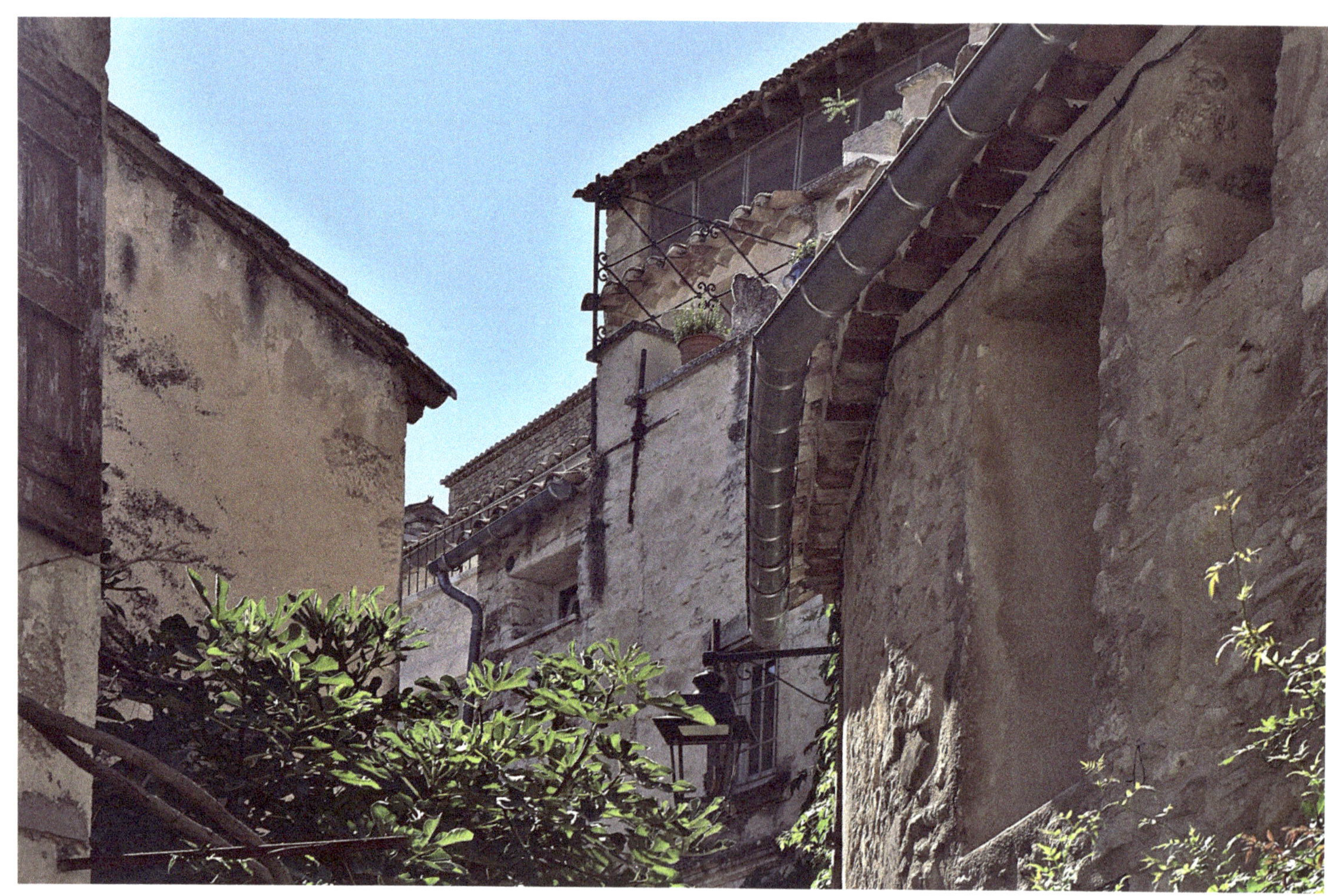

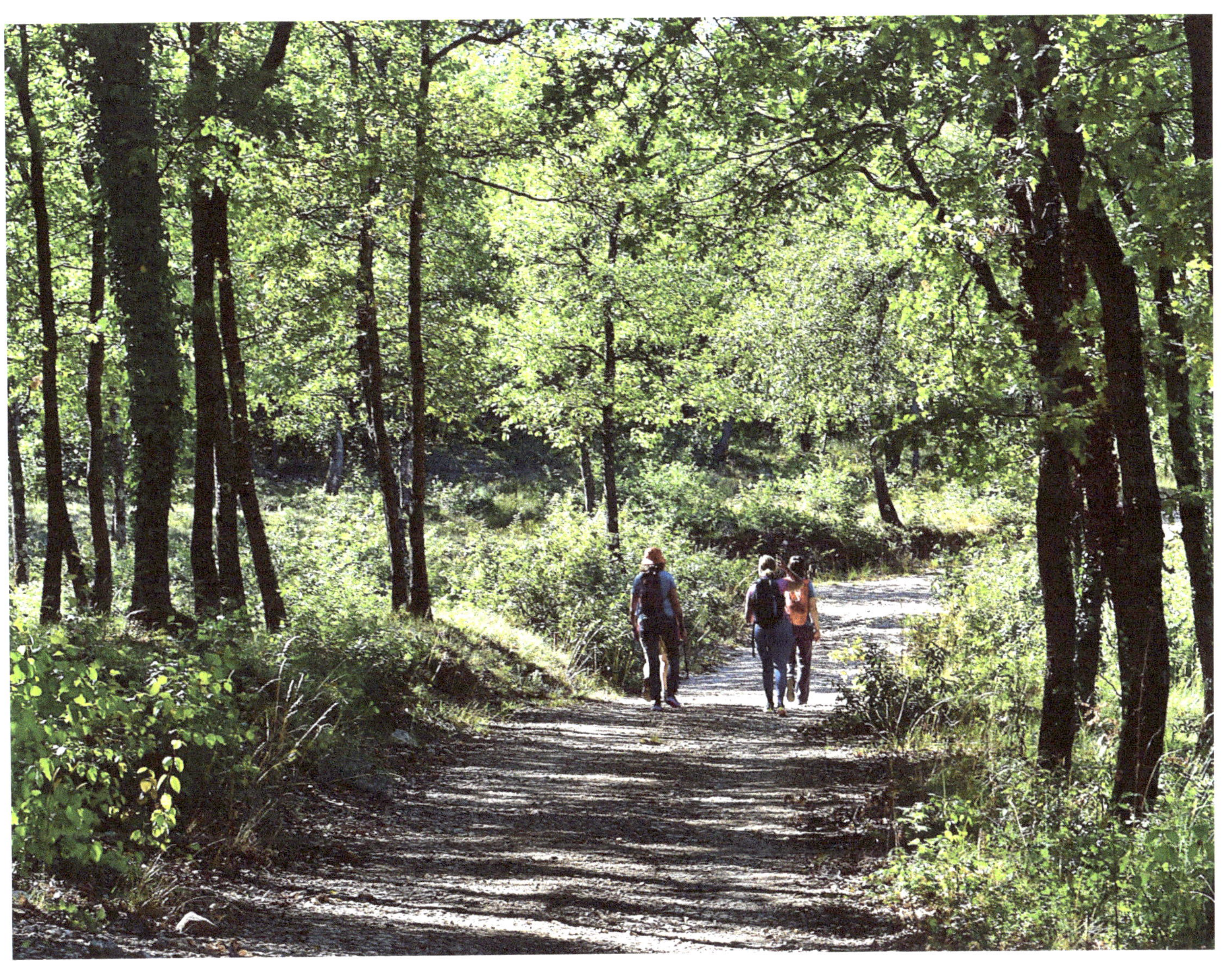

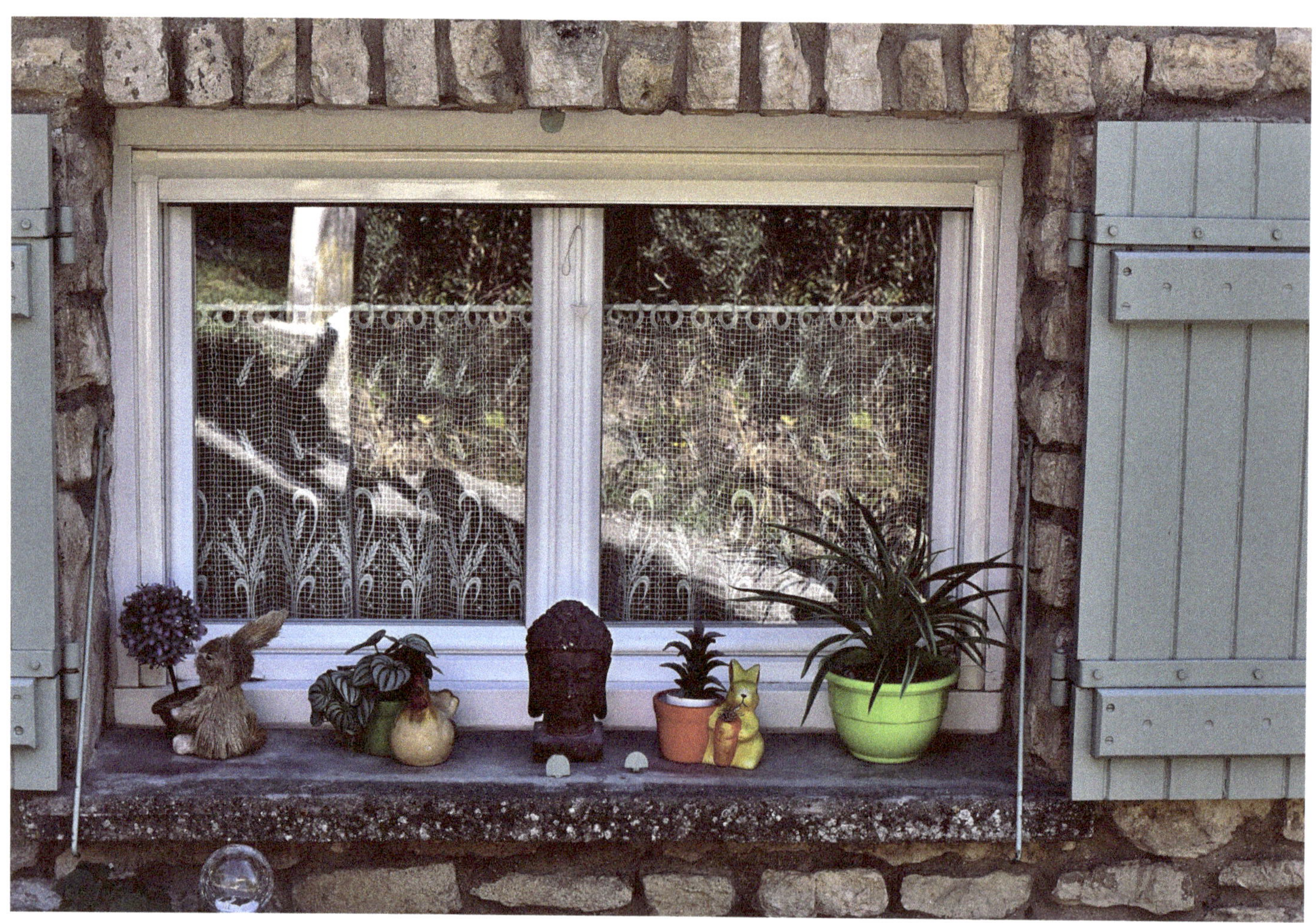

The mistral rises
To twirl and furl the cypress,
Swirl and curl the cross

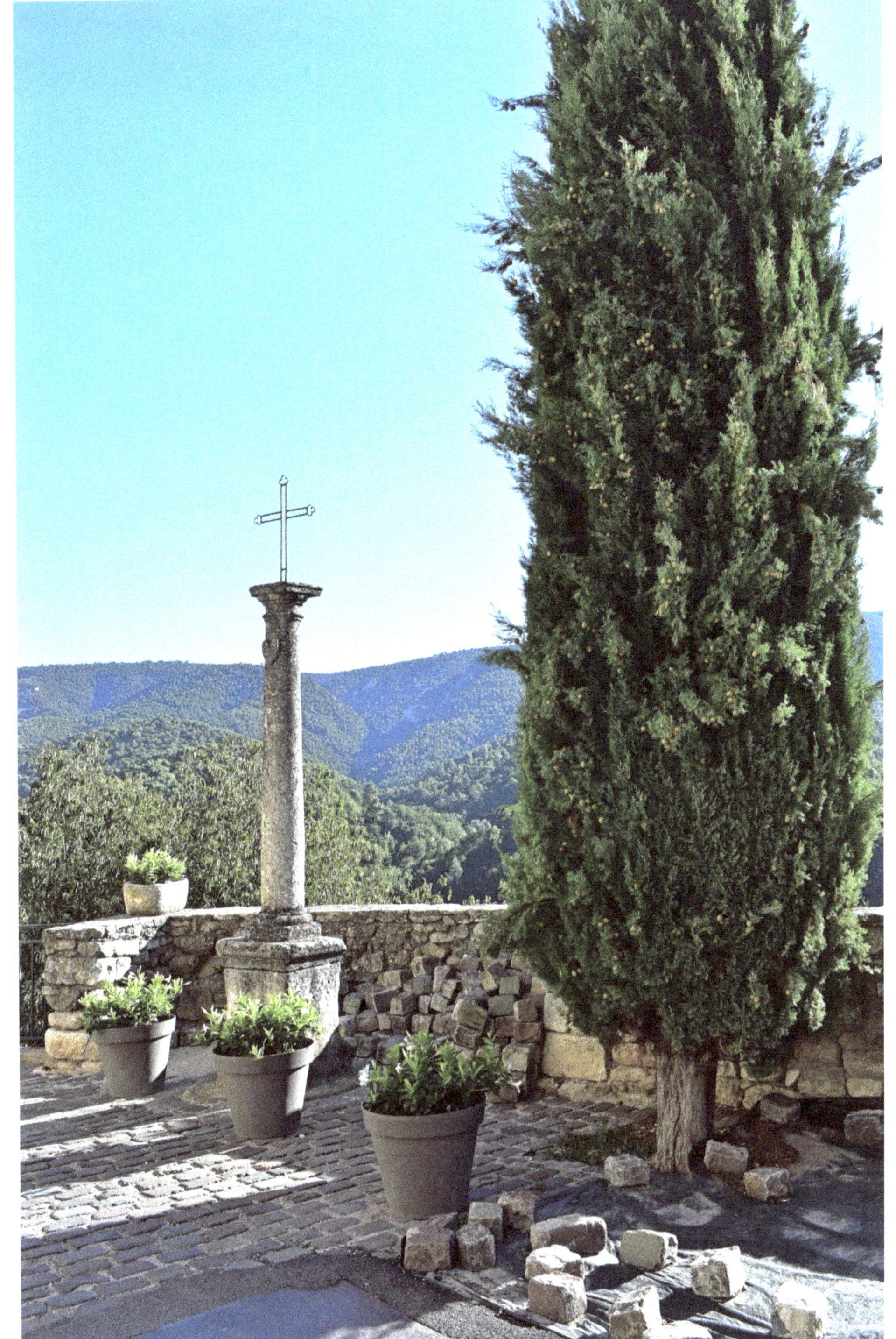

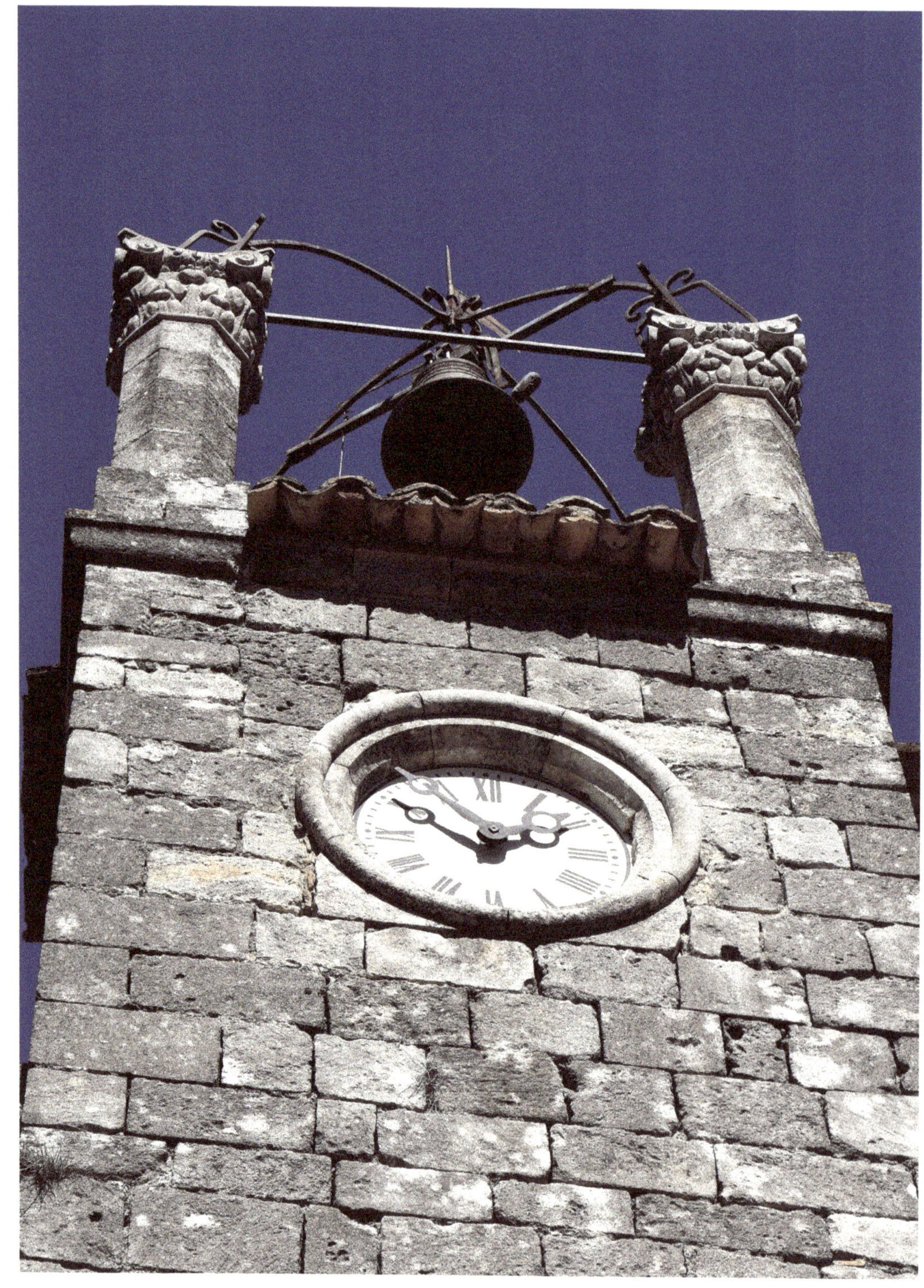

Chapter Two

86 Steps

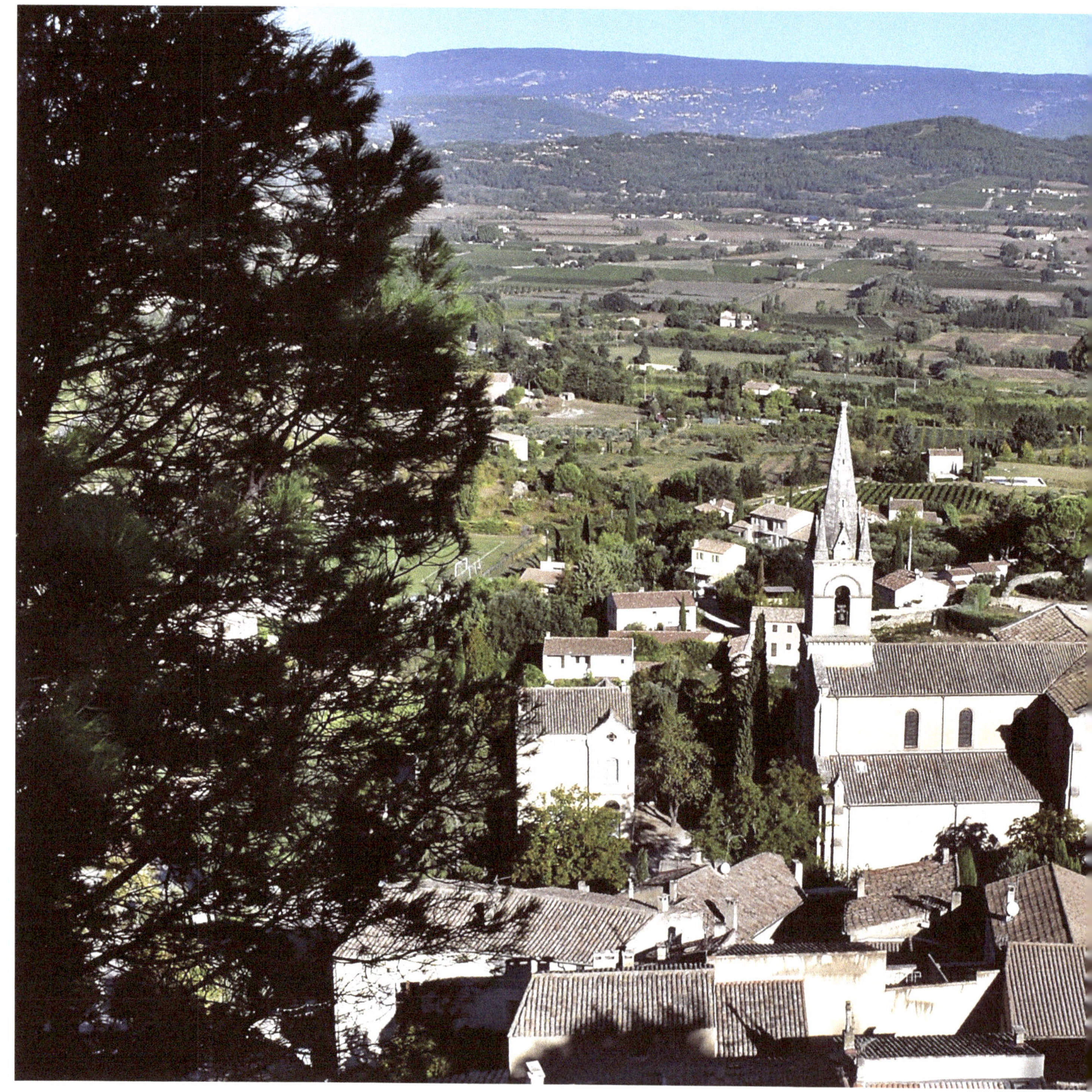

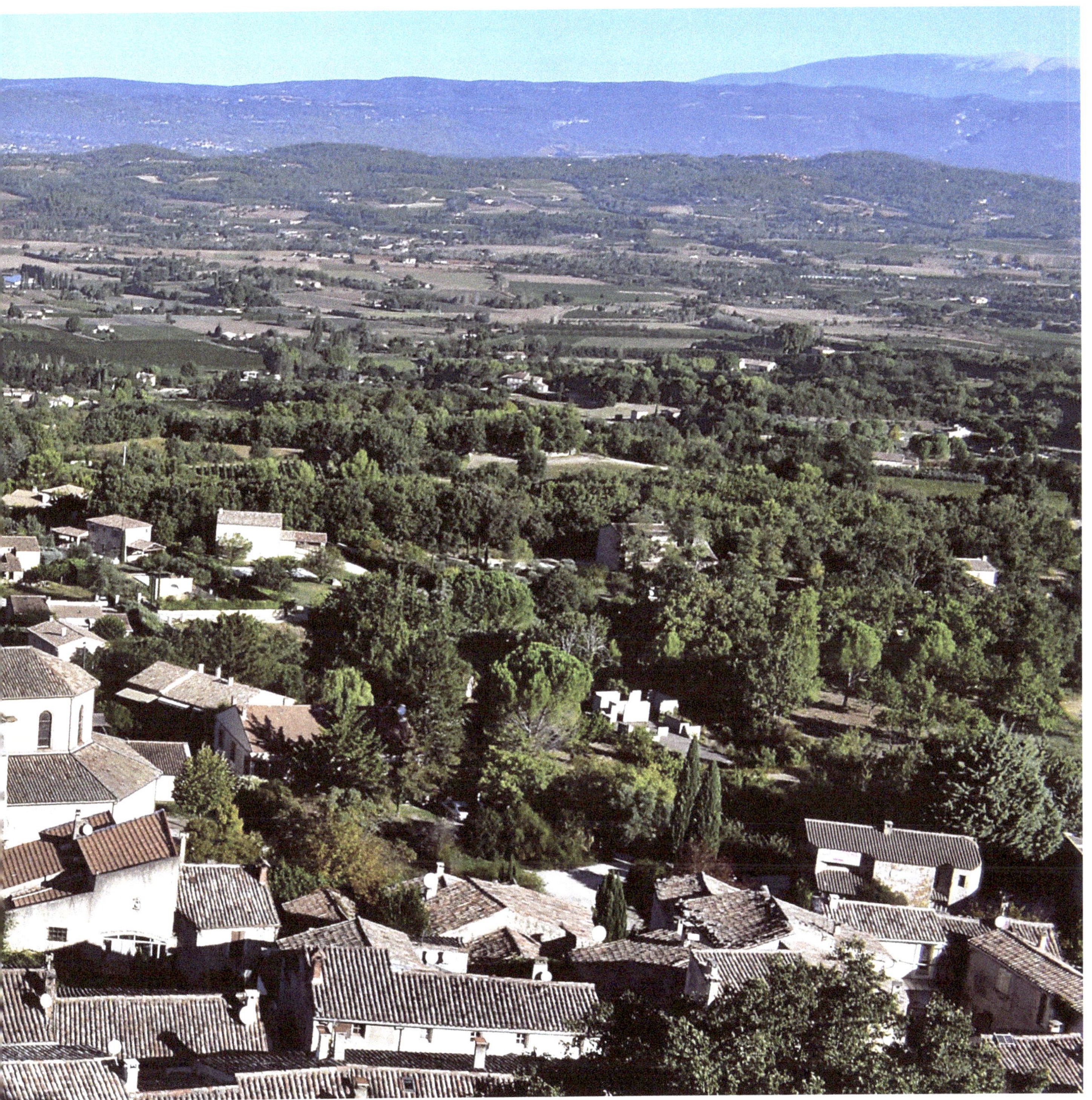

Bonnieux

We know so little about our Neanderthal cousins. They were like us in some ways, different in others. We know them physically from their fossil remains and can speculate about their lifestyle from other clues they left behind. We even know, from the traces of their DNA in our genes, that we had intimate relations with them that were, hopefully, enjoyable for both of us. What we don't know much about is their aesthetics. We have found bones and stones believed to have been decorated by them and abstract cave paintings that we attribute to them, but did they have a craving for beauty that could influence their selection of homesites? We can only speculate, but such a desire could explain their presence 60,000 years ago near Bonnieux.

Today, we climb the 86 stone steps to the Old Church and behold a panorama of plains patchworked with lush vineyards, stands of fruit trees, and fields of lavender and grain. When Neanderthals roamed the hilltop, they may not have seen fields and vineyards, but they would have beheld Mont Ventoux in the Vaucluse Mountains. Did our ancient cousins stop to stare in wonder, as we do ?

The monks who built the monastery in the sixth century almost certainly did, and eventually a community grew around them until a walled village arose on the hillside, to be followed in the 13th century by the Castellas, a seigneurial castle built by the powerful Agoult family, and by the Chapel St. Sauveur, built by the Templars. In the 14th century, the town became pontifical land and soon the residence of many bishops and other ecclesiastical dignitaries, men who appreciated the good things in life and congregated in places where they could be enjoyed.

By the 1700s, the village was a bustling, bodacious city with 3,500 inhabitants and views of the sister towns of Gordes and Roussillon across the valley. If they had still been around at the end of the 19th century, our Neanderthal brethren would have been astounded by their neighborhood. The village was the home to 18 bistros, six gambling rooms, and two brothels. Panoramic views were not the only indulgent pleasures of Bonnieux.

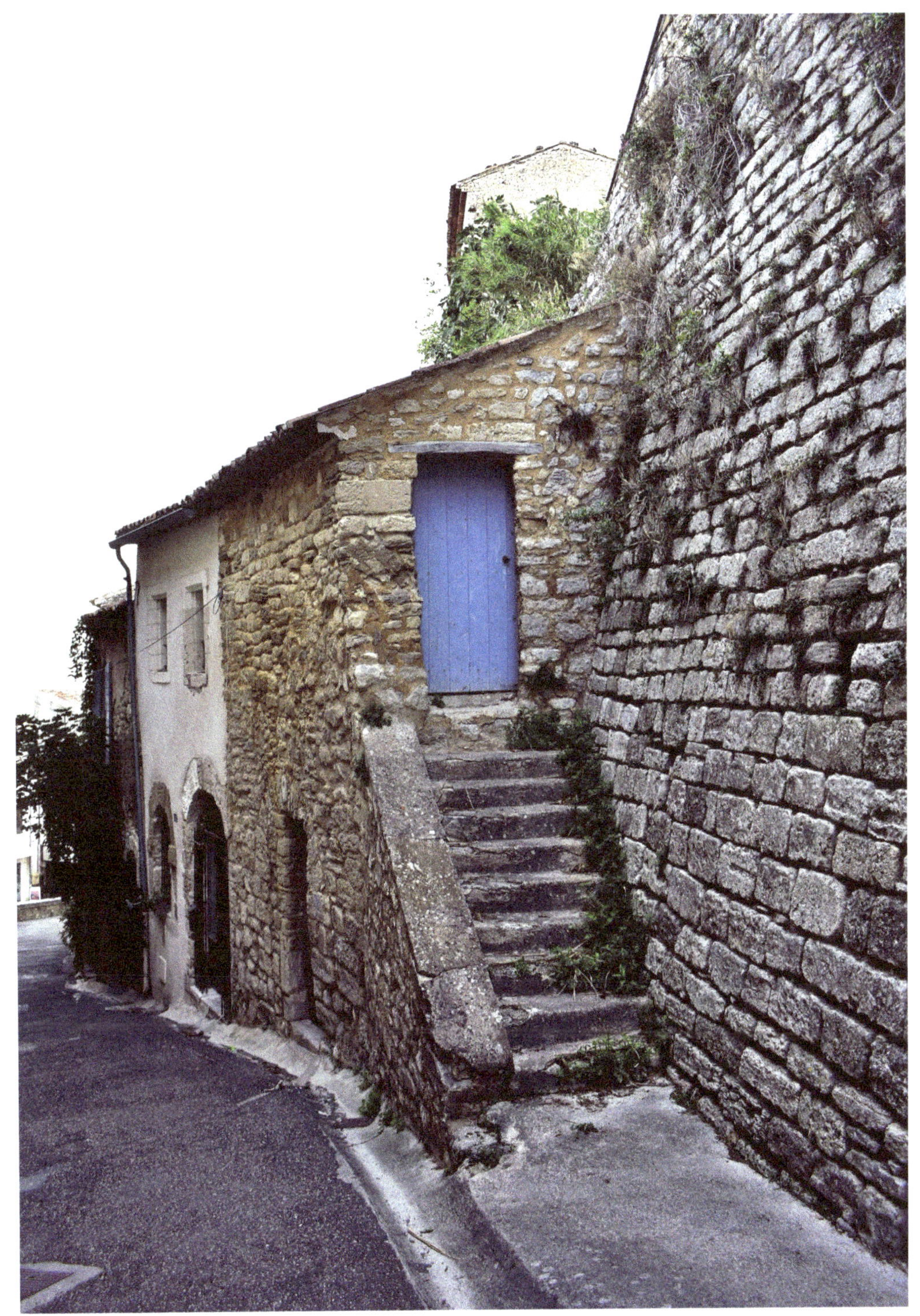

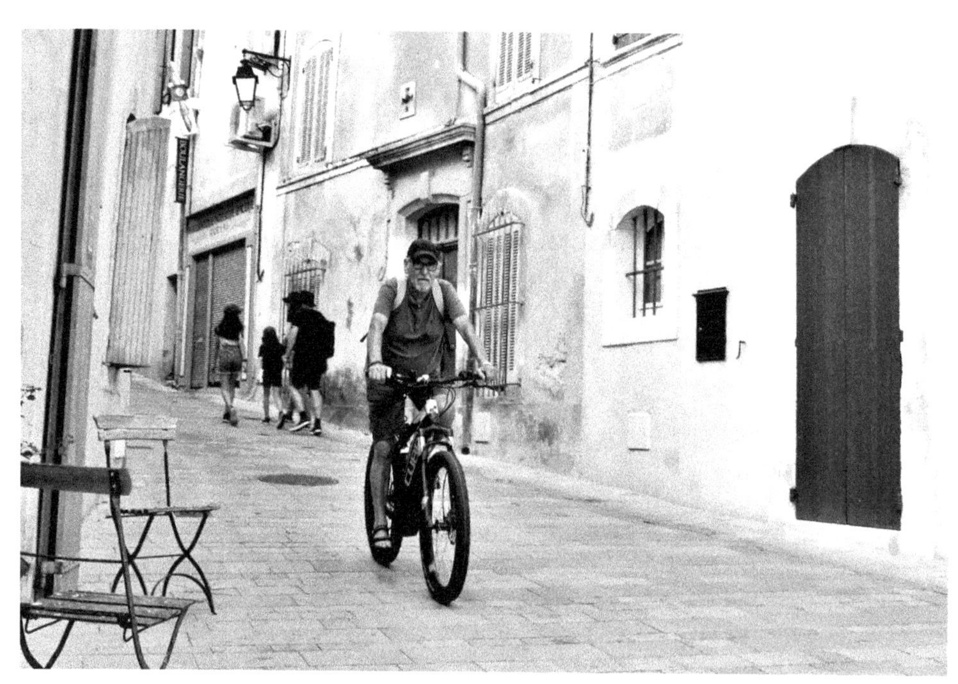
BOULANGERIE

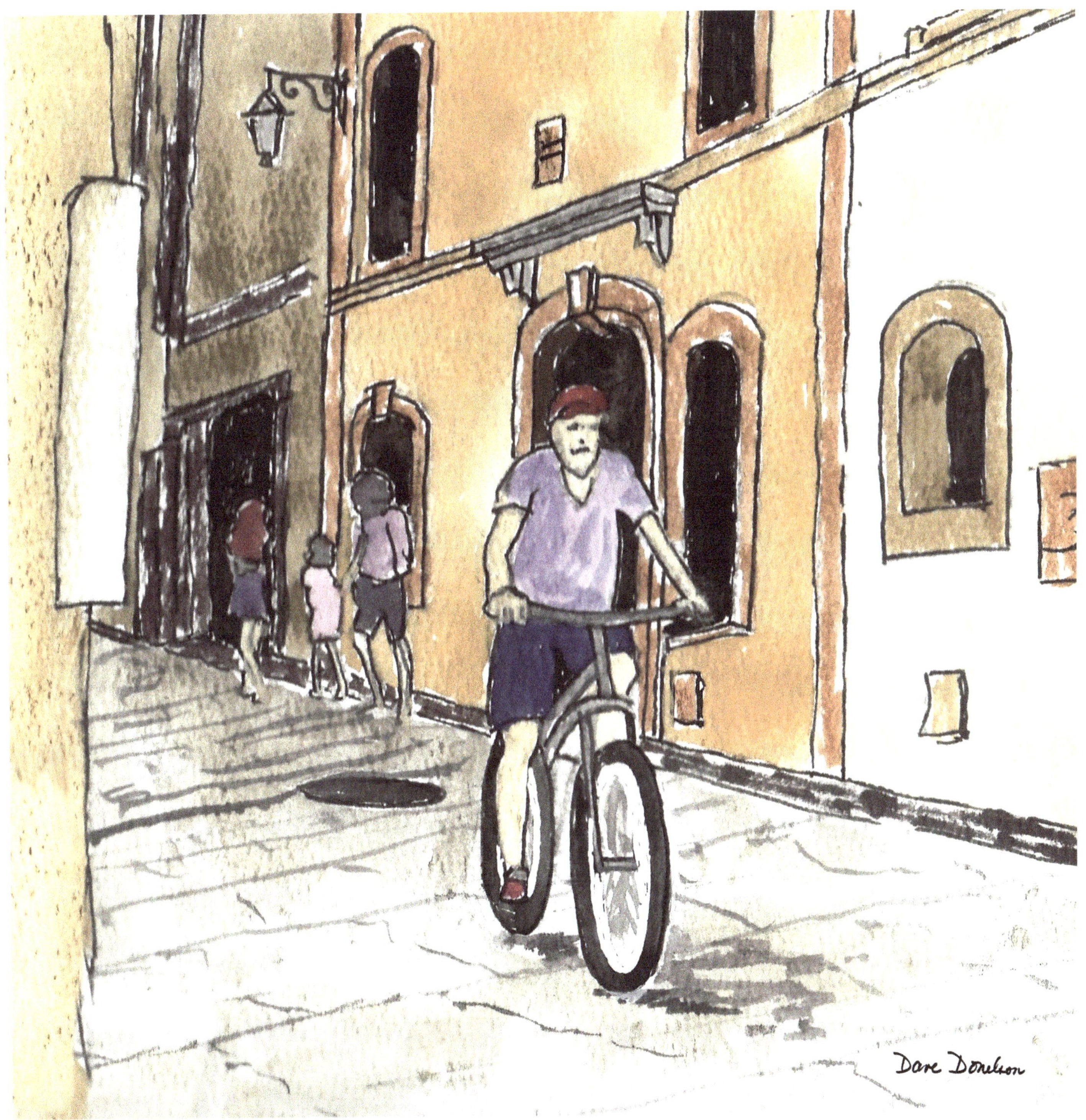
Dave Donelson

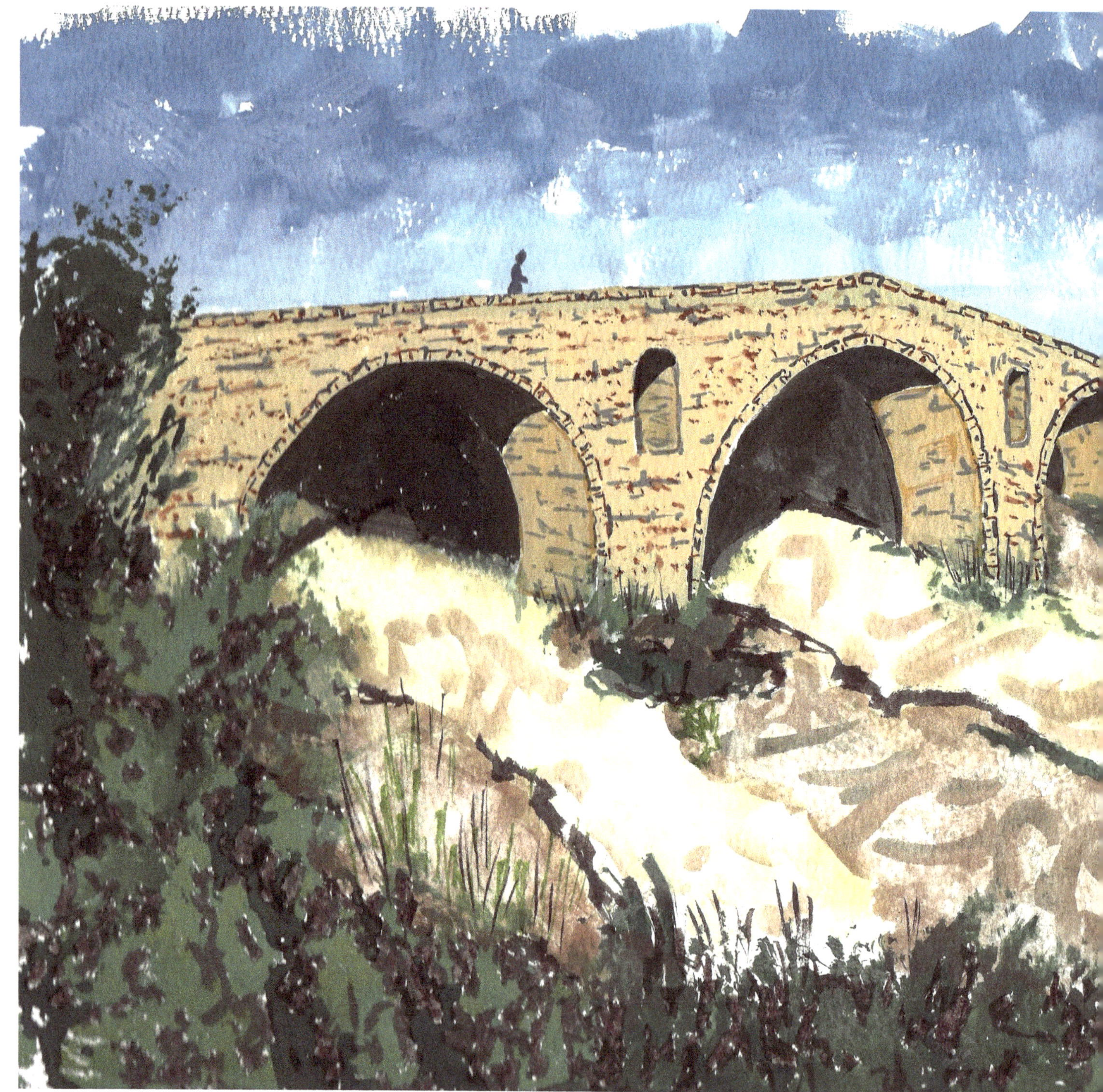

Ode to Pont Julien

I

Three true arches lift Pont Julien
Over the eddies and tumbling flows
Of the mountain river Calavan.

The impassive bridge ignores the stream
Rippling around its wet stoney toes;
Disregards the walkers on its spine.

The rushing rising waters of spring
Would wash away the bridge but for the
Clever tunnels between the arches.

Via Domitia spans the bridge
From bank to bank on cobbled roadbed,
A viaduct to last forever.

One day, while hiking the ancient road,
I cross the bridge and stop to ponder
Its place in our human history.

When travelers once came here like me,
They heard the clonk of oxen hooves and
The hard rumbling of iron-clad wheels,

The sharp cries and whistles of drovers,
The cadenced trampling of legionnaires,
The crack of the lash on beast and slave.

At first, I marveled at how the bridge
Mirrored the graceful curve of far hills
Rising slow against the horizon.

Born before Christ, after Julius,
The bridge stood steadfast two thousand years
Before I divined its brutal song.

II

The empire's engineers knew science,
The math of force and friction and mass,
But it was workmanship that mattered.

Slaves with chisels cut each perfect stone,
Endless ones shaped to lay together,
Angled to form the graceful arches,

Carefully carved by hard hands skilled with
Mallet and chisel, iron wedge and maul,
Standing without mortar, bound by blood.

"Gallia est omnis divisa
In partes tres," wrote the man for whom
The bridge was named after he was killed.

He led men across the continent
To gain power, glory, and acclaim
Only to lose it all in the end.

Julius became a god of Rome,
A head on a coin, a man in song
Whose minions wielded the bitter lash.

After Caesar's death in the Senate,
Before Christ's birth and execution,
Pont Julien had a history.

Knots of scars on the backs of the slaves
Told the horror of their existence,
Gave lie the cruel myth of free will.

Empire was built death on death on death.
The bridge was built stone on stone on stone.
My legacy: word on word on word.

III

I transverse the bridge in but minutes,
Measure the cobbles beneath my soles,
Trace the agonies of the masons.

I lay marks on paper carefully,
Each chosen with deliberation
To fit tight with others on the page,

Snug in place, solid in idea.
They brace each other to support thought
Meant to last like Luberon limestone.

His words could not stop the assassins.
Nor could they protect Rome from the Goths
My words have the same futility.

Marks I make today will disappear.
I have no delusions on that score.
They are not stone quarried to endure.

My hand holds a lash that drives my work
In hopes it will last long enough
To sing its song to someone somewhere.

I trail my fingers along the wall
Thinking about the men who built it.
No plaque honors their brief stolen lives.

They are not mentioned in histories.
Their names—if any—are forgotten.
The bridge does not bear their signature.

Unless this rune I see carved in stone,
Hidden where the roadbed meets the wall,
Is their cry for forlorn remembrance.

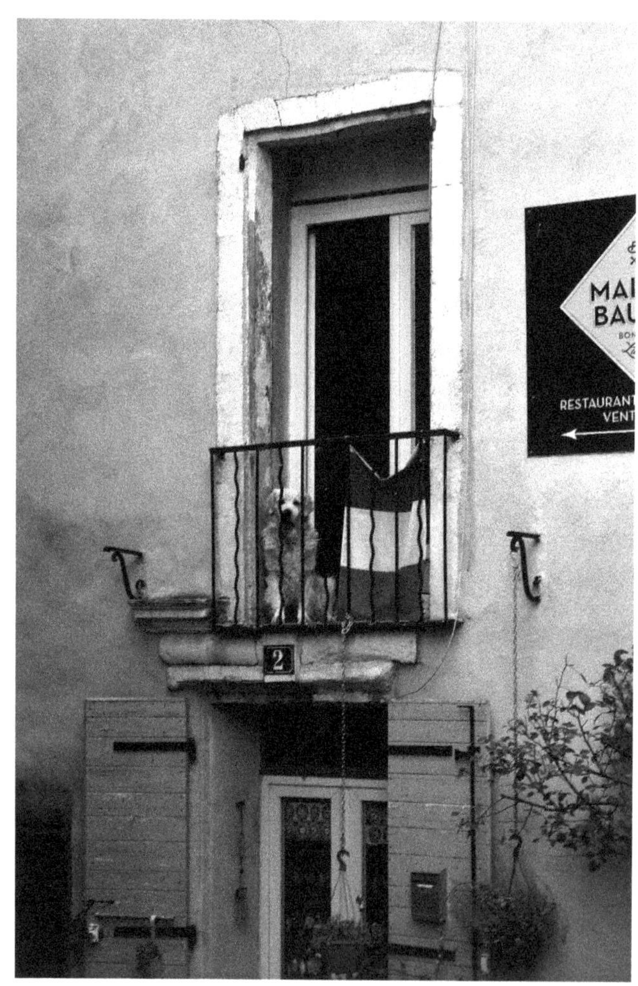
RESTAURANT
2

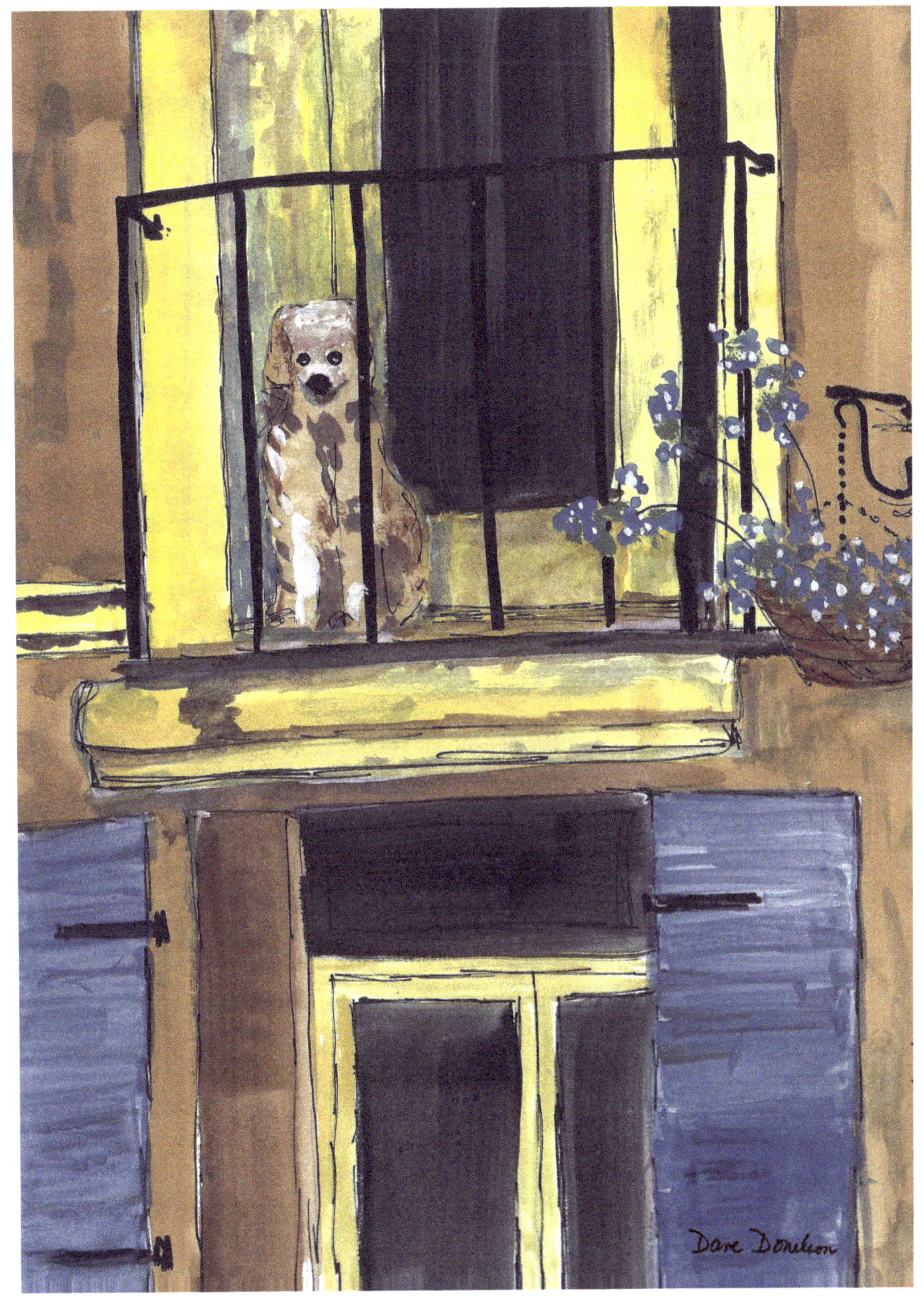
Dave Donelson

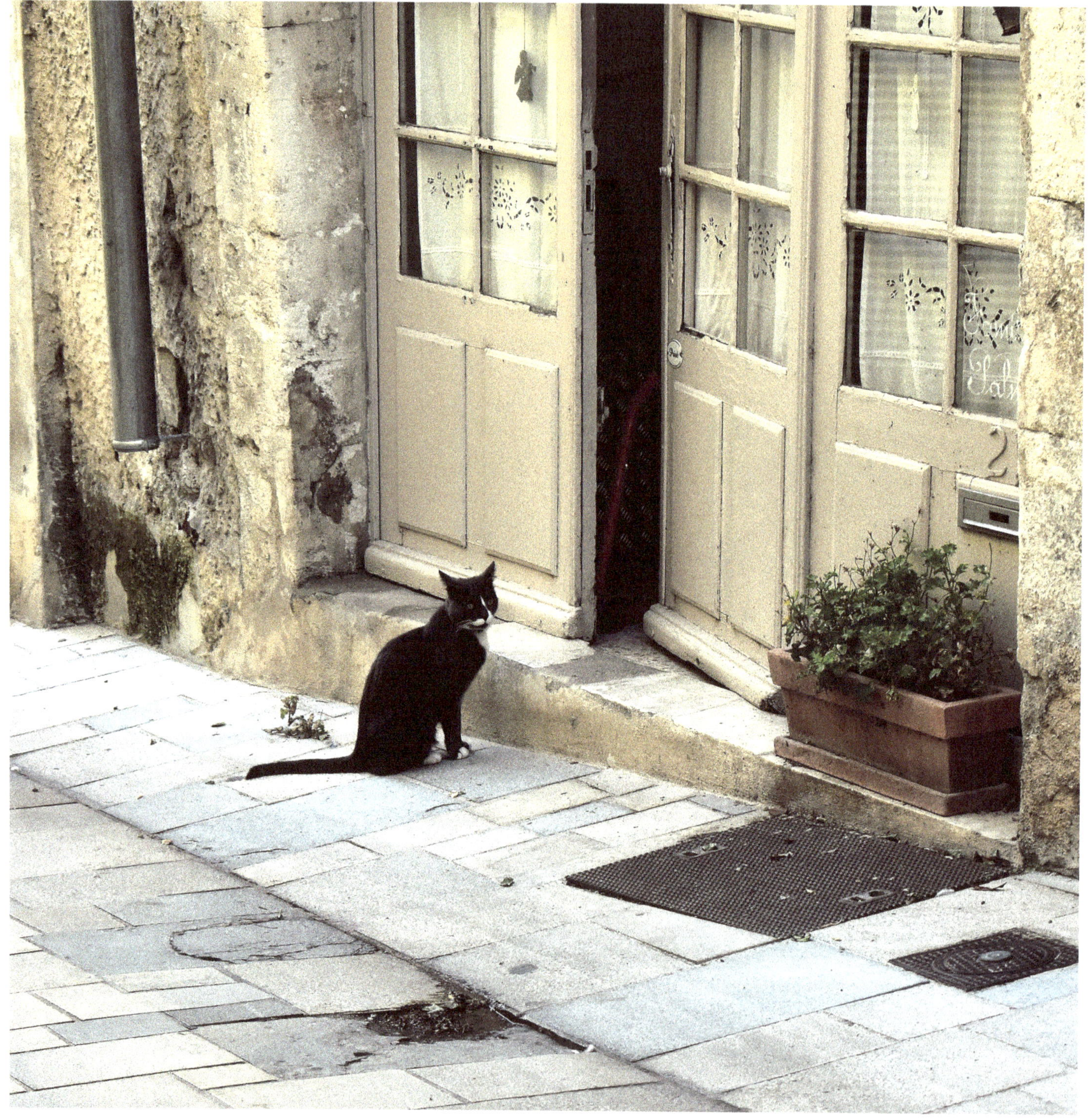

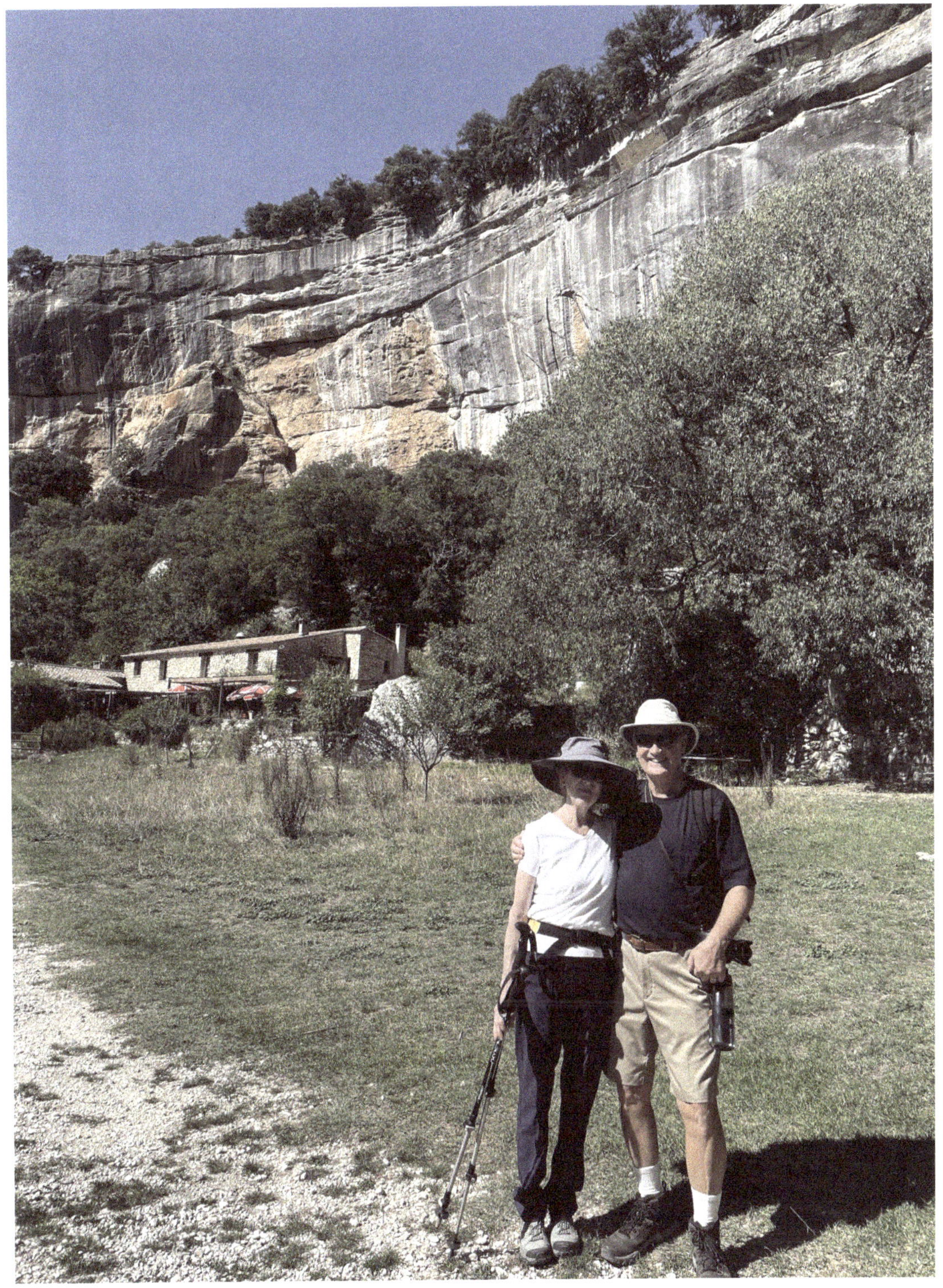

The Carriere

Jews, stereotyped as manipulative merchants and merciless moneylenders, were condemned to dwell beneath contempt in tunnel caves dark and dank. It is a story as old as the Romans but given new life when, in1348, the Black Death struck the world and the Jews were accused of poisoning the wells to spread the epidemic for their economic and social benefit.

Antisemitic violence continued through the fifteenth century until various edicts were issued to expel the Jews from the region. Those few who remained were grouped into *carrieres,* or ghettoes, that were gated and locked at night. Jews were ordered to wear identifying yellow hats and prohibited from owning property other than their dwellings. They were disqualified from professional occupations and, as merchants, they were allowed to sell only secondhand items. They lived under these abhorrent conditions until well into the 18th century, when a few professions, mercantile occupations, and money-lending were allowed.

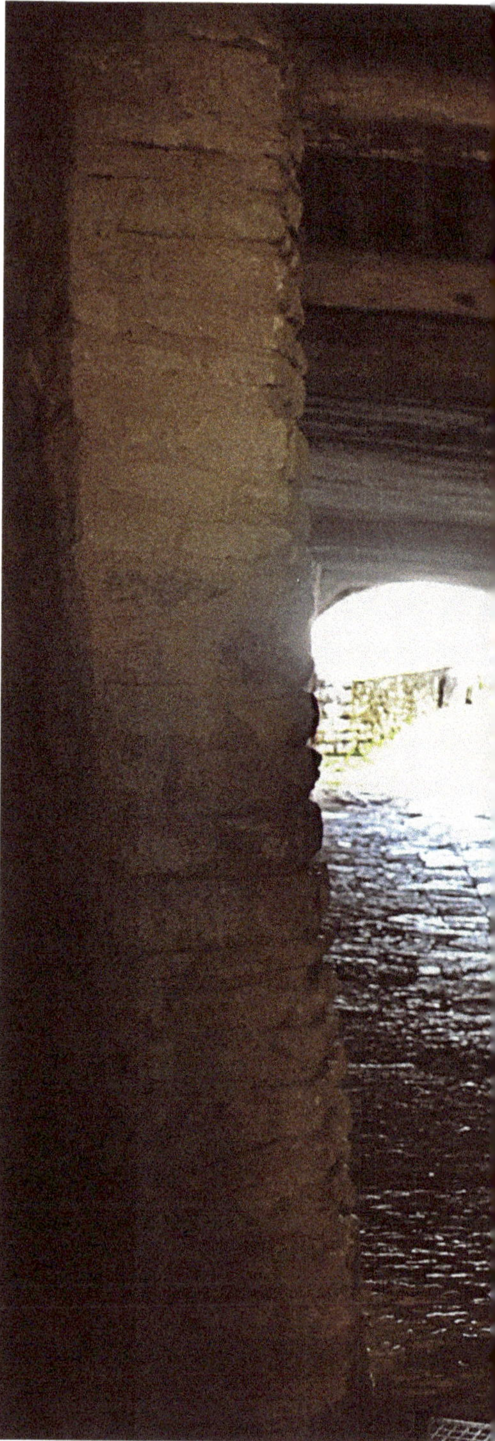

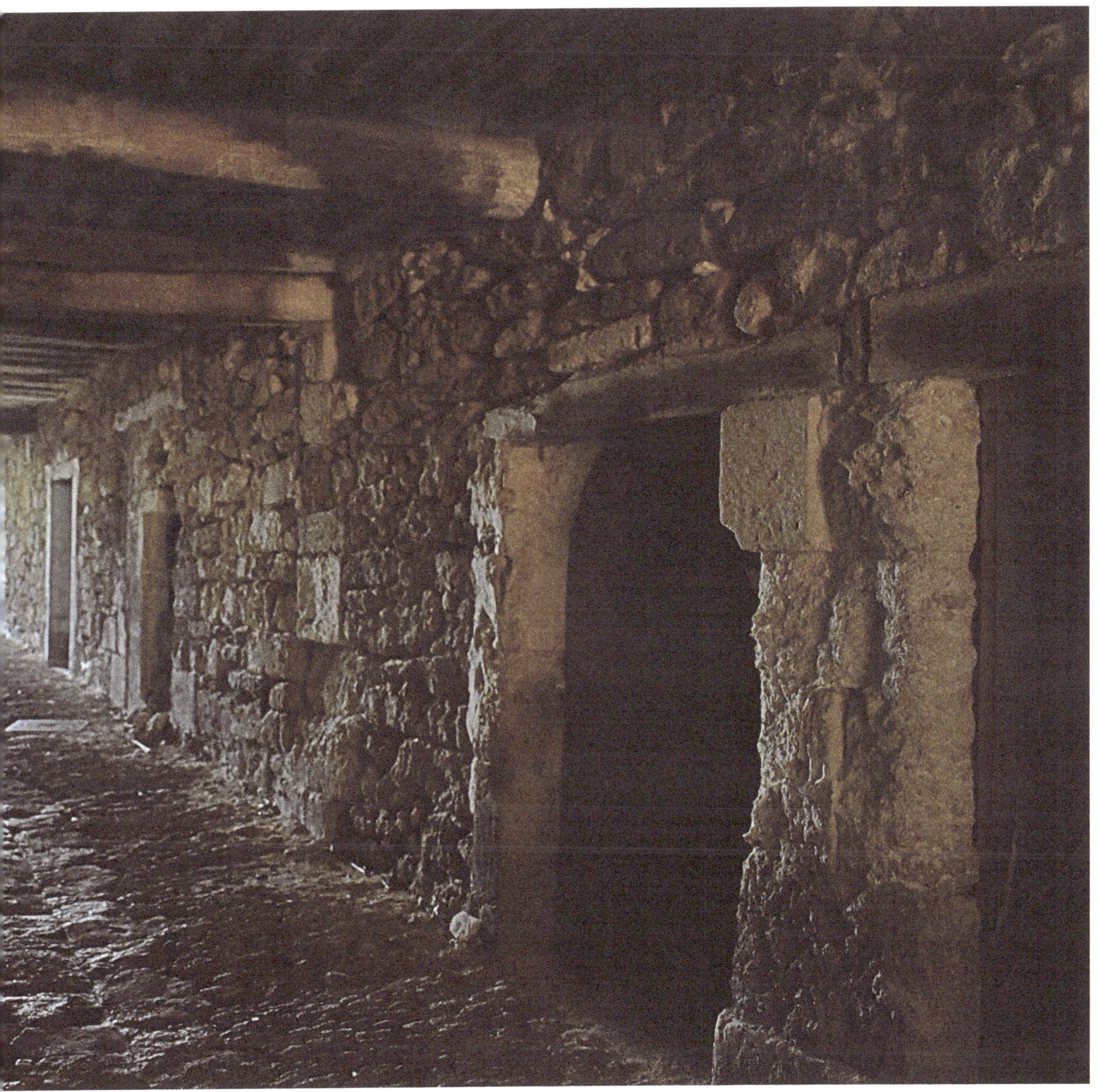

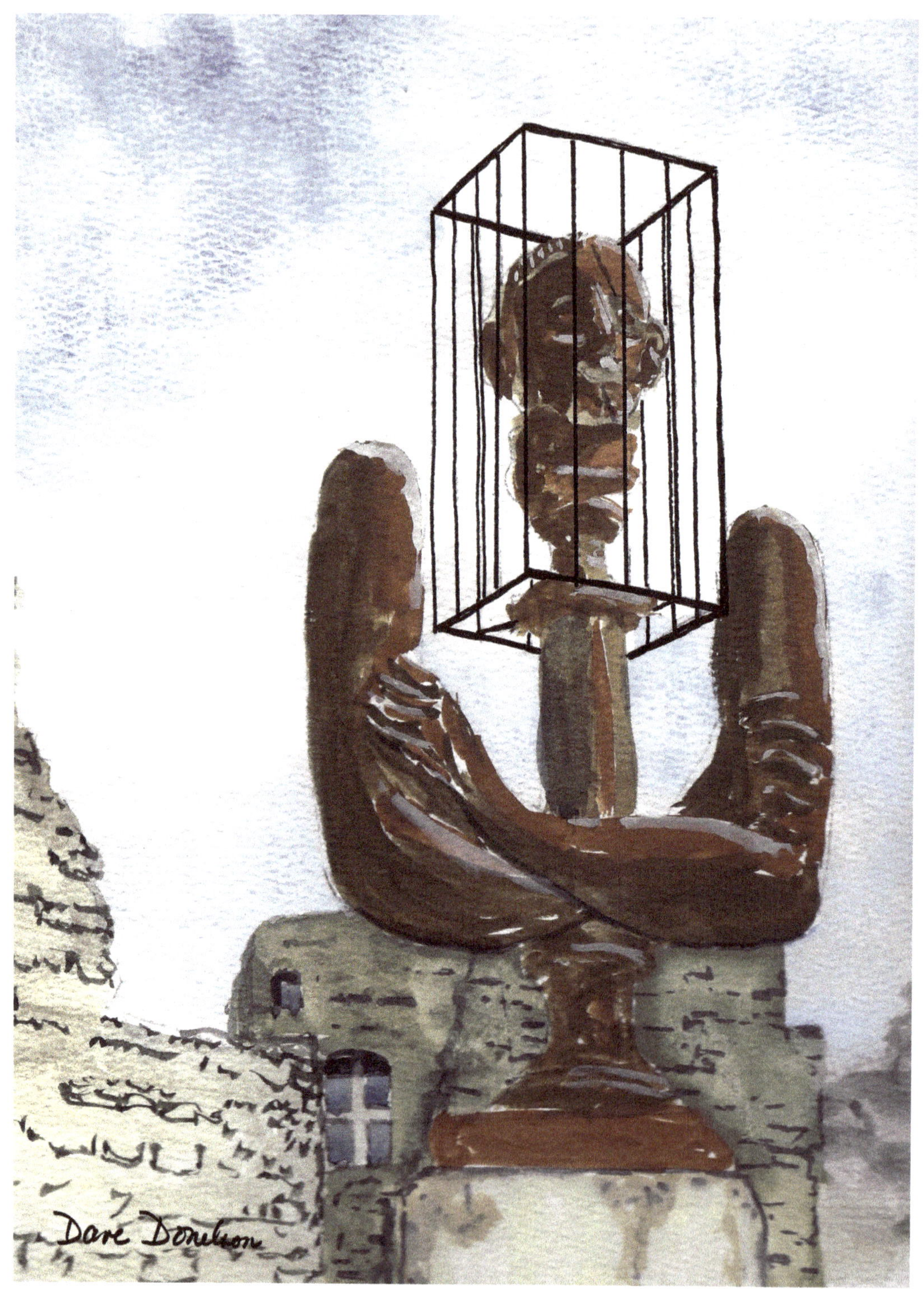
Dave Donelson

Chapter Three
Beauty and Pain

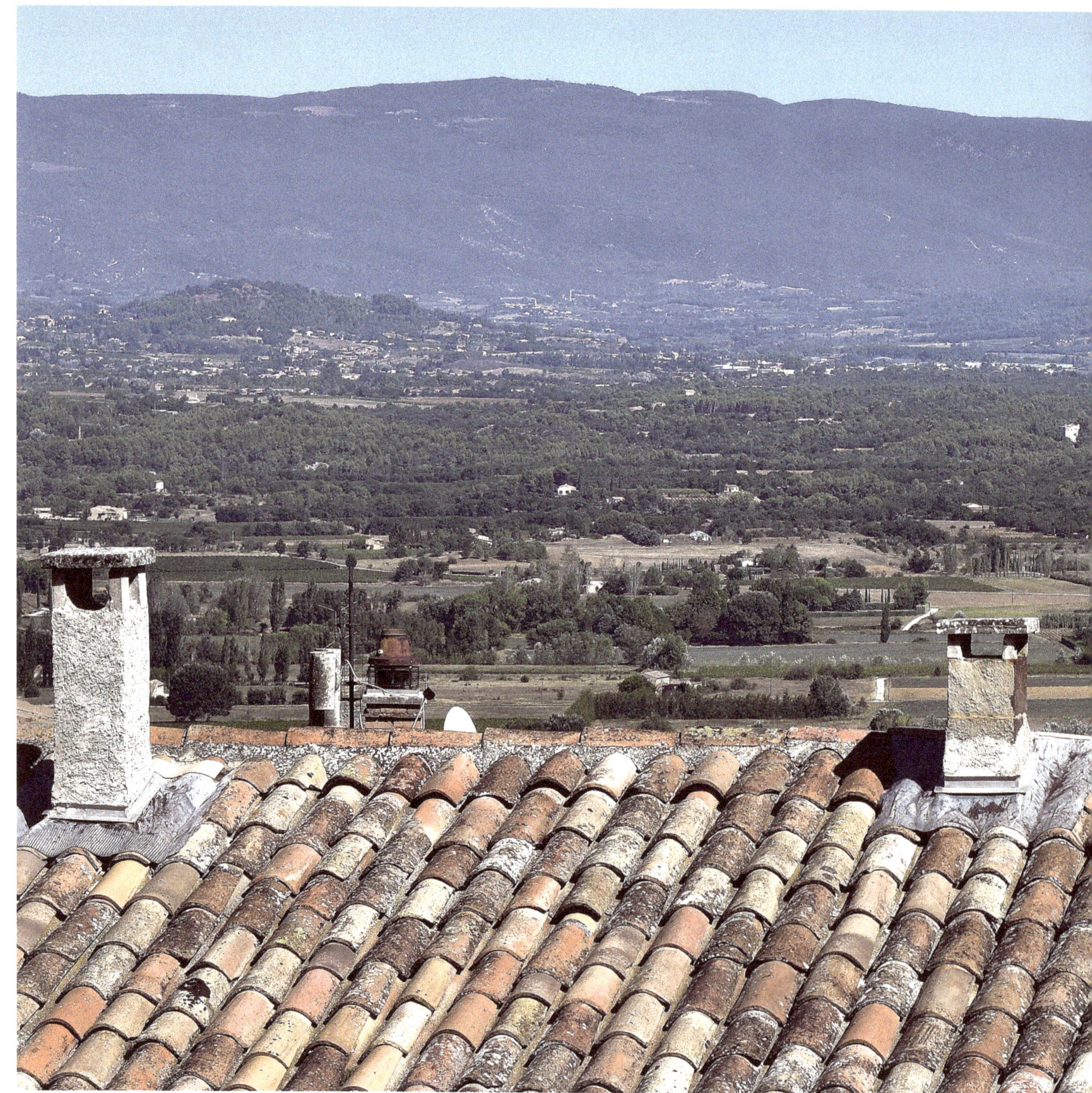

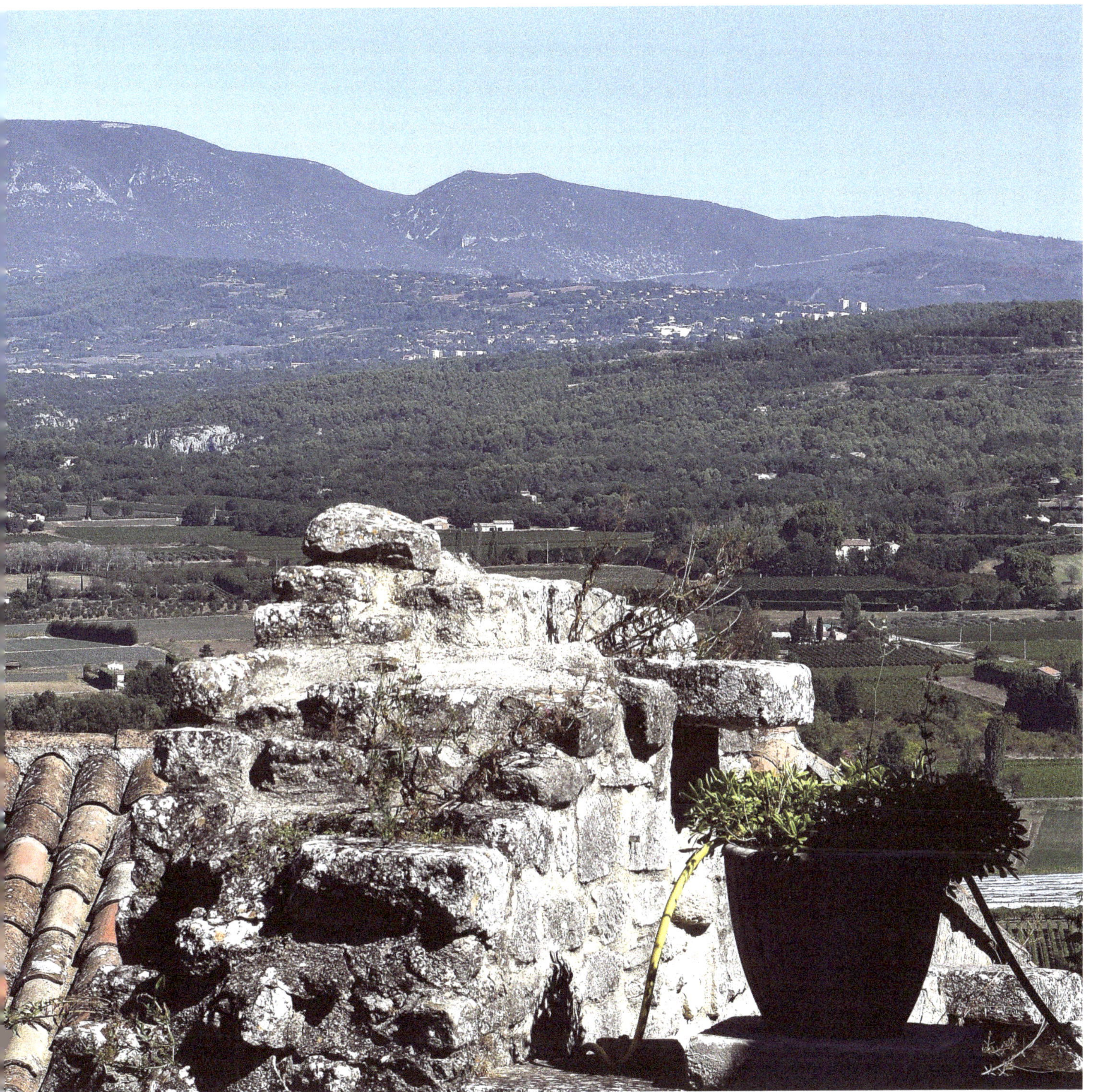

Lacoste

Artists can be inspired by horror as well as beauty. The art engendered by those muses reminds us that both have always existed—and always will.

The infamous Marquis de Sade is unfailingly cited as the reprehensible figurehead of Lacoste, but the village was the scene of bloody events long before his family built a castle on the hill. During the 14th century, the village suffered so greatly from plague, wars, and banditry that it came close to disappearing and the few remaining residents recruited the Waldensians to move in, which they did. Unfortunately, these Christian reformers were considered heretics by the Catholic Church.

In 1545, the Maynier d'Oppede mounted a campaign to destroy this afront to papal authority under orders of the Parliament of Aix. When he was stopped by the defenders at the gates of Lacoste, he persuaded them he would spare their lives if they let him in. He lied. Once admitted, his men pillaged the village, raped the women, and massacred every single inhabitant.

By the time de Sade arrived on the scene years later, the tiny village was once again inhabited, although not by a sedate, placid populace. The villagers ran the marquis out of town and into prison after a series of ugly incidents with local women and the police. They partially destroyed his castle in 1779.

Lacoste today has left its bloody past behind and become a center of the arts. The Lacoste School of the Arts was founded in 1970 by American painter Bernard Pfriem. Notable artists such as photographer Henri Cartier-Bresson and poet Gustaf Sobin came to Lacoste to work and teach. The school was later incorporated into the Savannah College of Art and Design (SCAD).

Fashion mogul Pierre Cardin purchased de Sade's dilapidated castle in the early 1990's and turned the attached quarry into a massive outdoor performance venue that today hosts an annual summer festival of world-class opera, theater, and music.

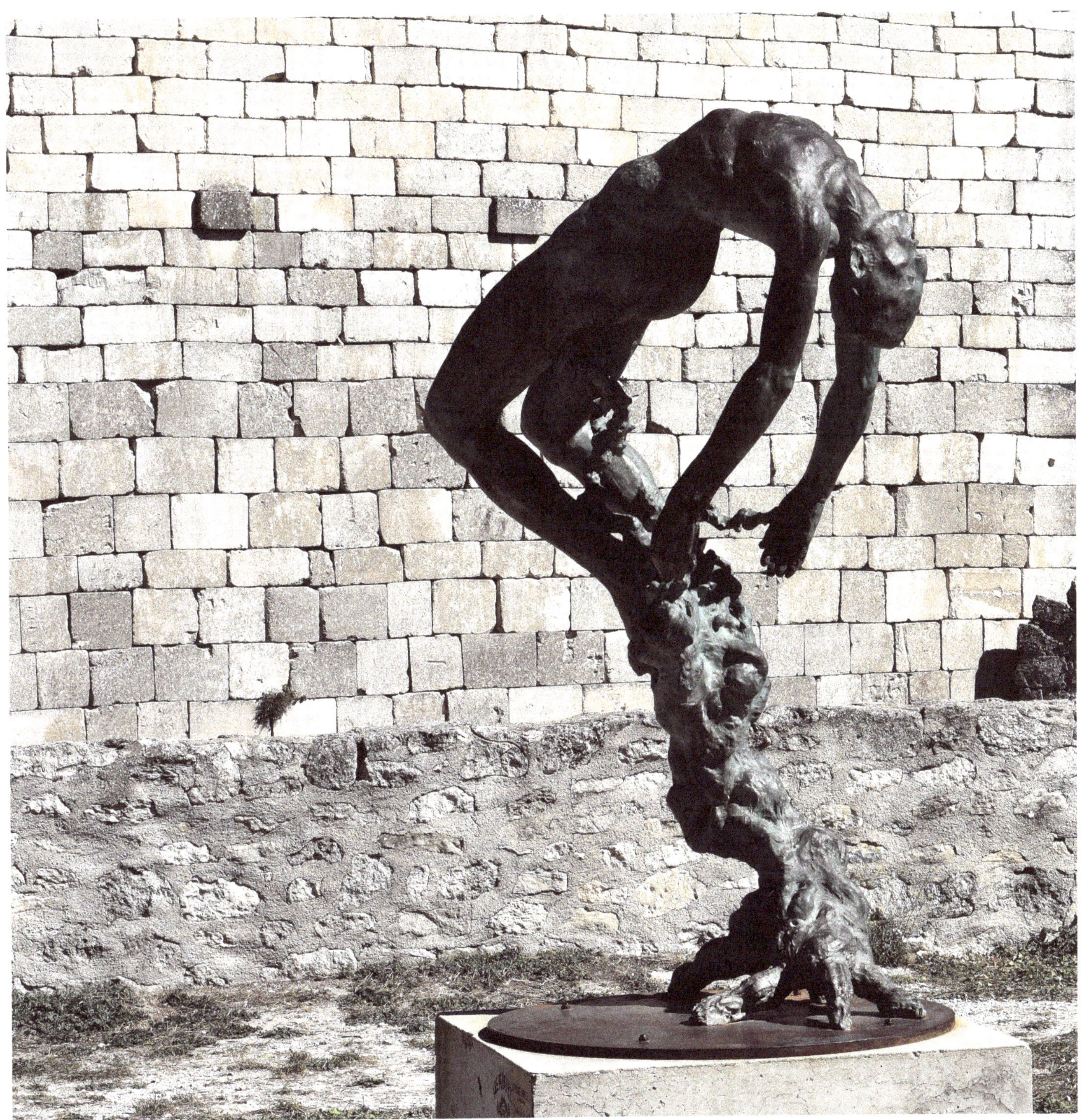

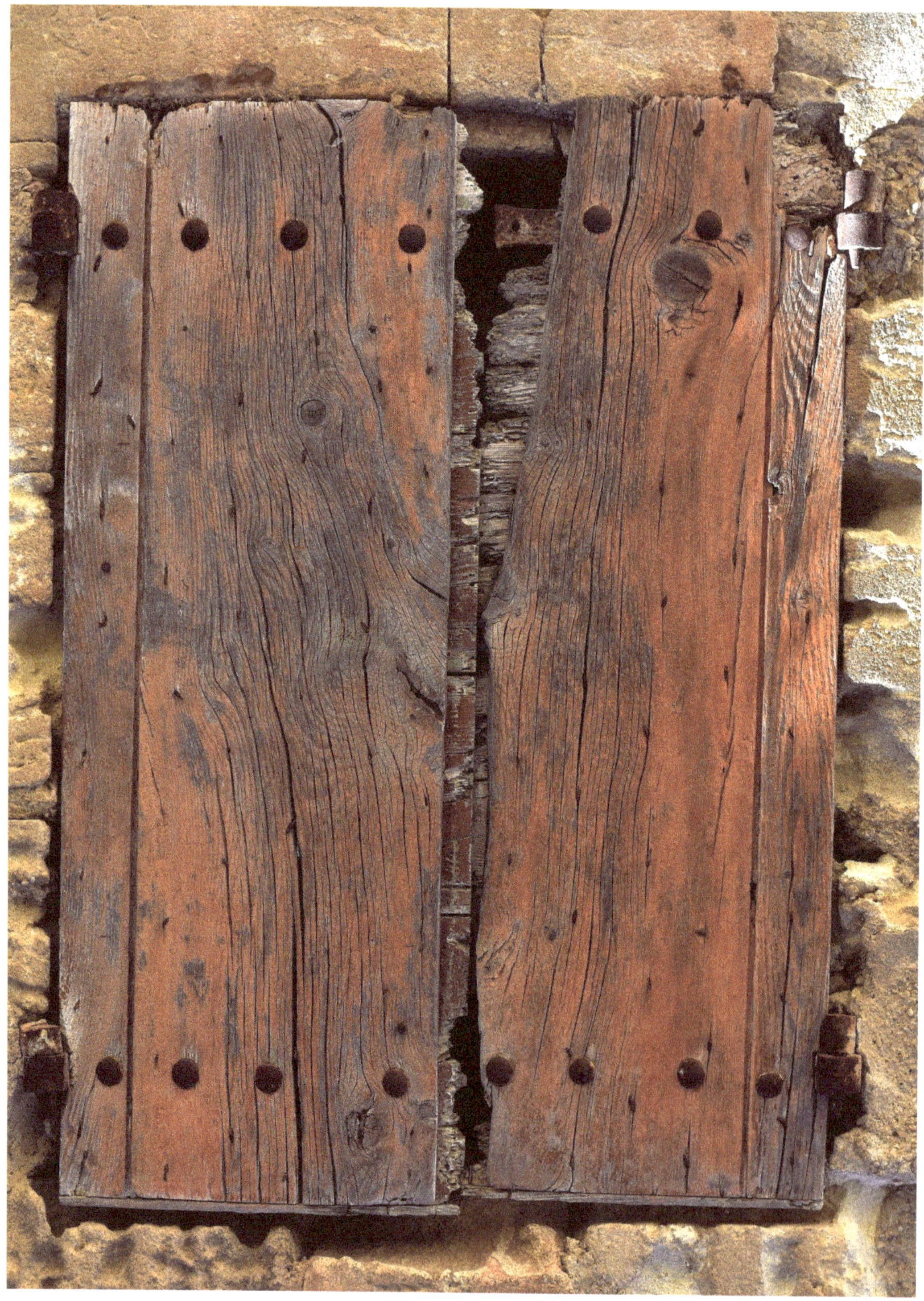

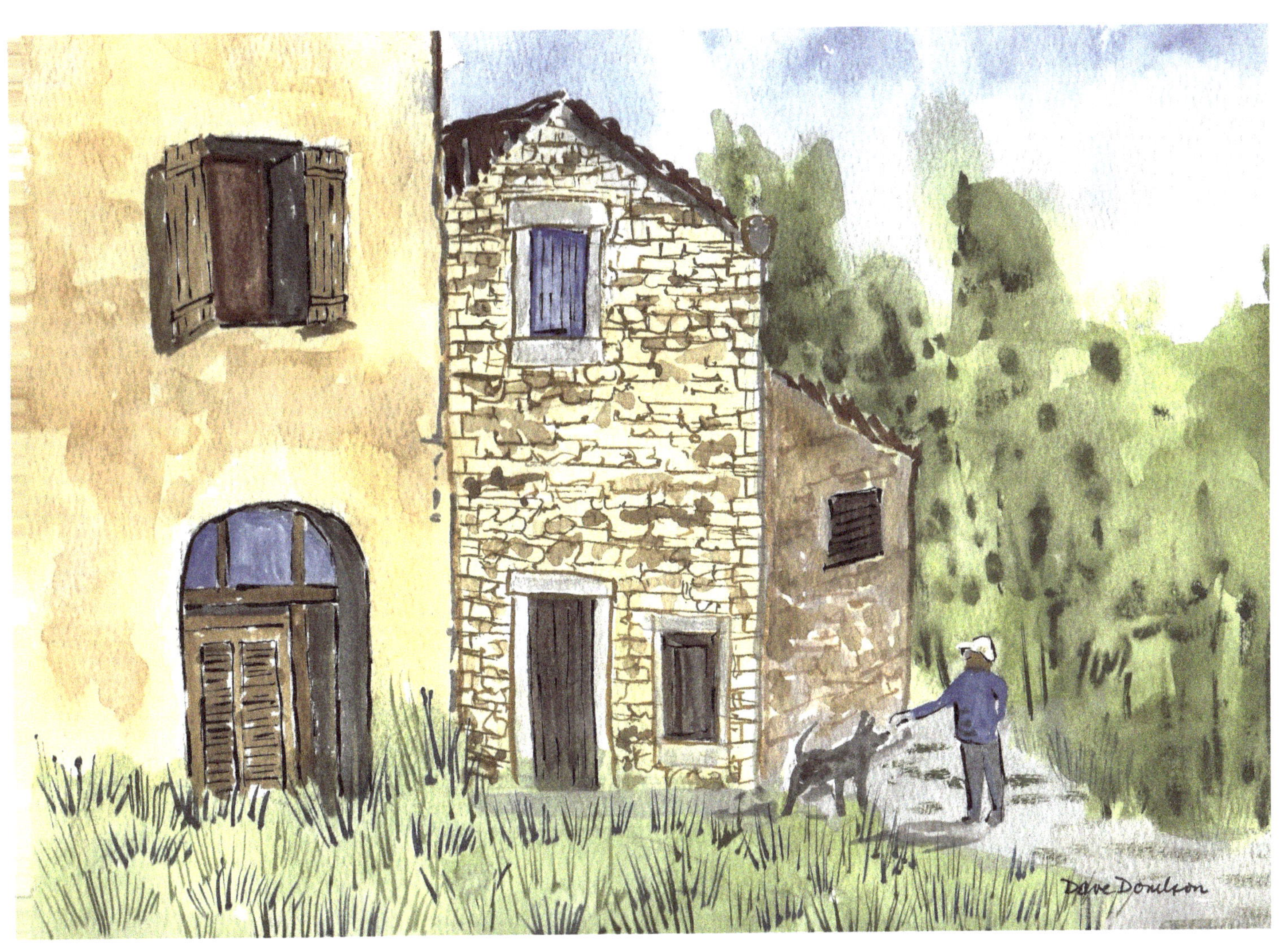

Scene Seen in the Chateau

The Chateau de Lacoste is the mostly-ruined former home of a man known by the title he inherited, the Marquis de Sade. The structure was set afire and largely destroyed during the French Revolution by villagers who detested de Sade for his aristocratic demeanor, not to mention the ignominy he brought to their town. Also because they wanted to use the limestone from which his chateau was made to build nice homes for themselves. Since the chateau stood on the top of the mountain, it was easy to knock down a fire-blacked wall or two and roll the stones downhill to use for other purposes. *Liberte, Egalite, Fraternite*, and all that.

Centuries later, the chateau was purchased and partially restored by another man famous for his thoughts about women's bodies, the fashion designer/mogul Pierre Cardin. The chateau commands a magnificent view of the Luberon valley and Cardin commissioned several pieces of statuary for the grounds to become part of that view. He was a man compelled to decide what others saw, whether it be on a woman's body or against the far horizon. Like de Sade, he believed himself above humanity's mediocrity.

What would happen if Cardin communed with the spirit of de Sade? What would they say to each other? Would de Sade comment on the statue of himself with his head mounted in a cage that Cardin put in the courtyard? Would Cardin inquire as to why de Sade built a theater? Would de Sade make some suggestions on how the theater could be used when Cardin was the only member of the audience? Or the star of the show? The possible topics are endless, especially considering how their attitudes toward women were similar, one hidden by the curtain of commerce, the other notoriously and openly malevolent.

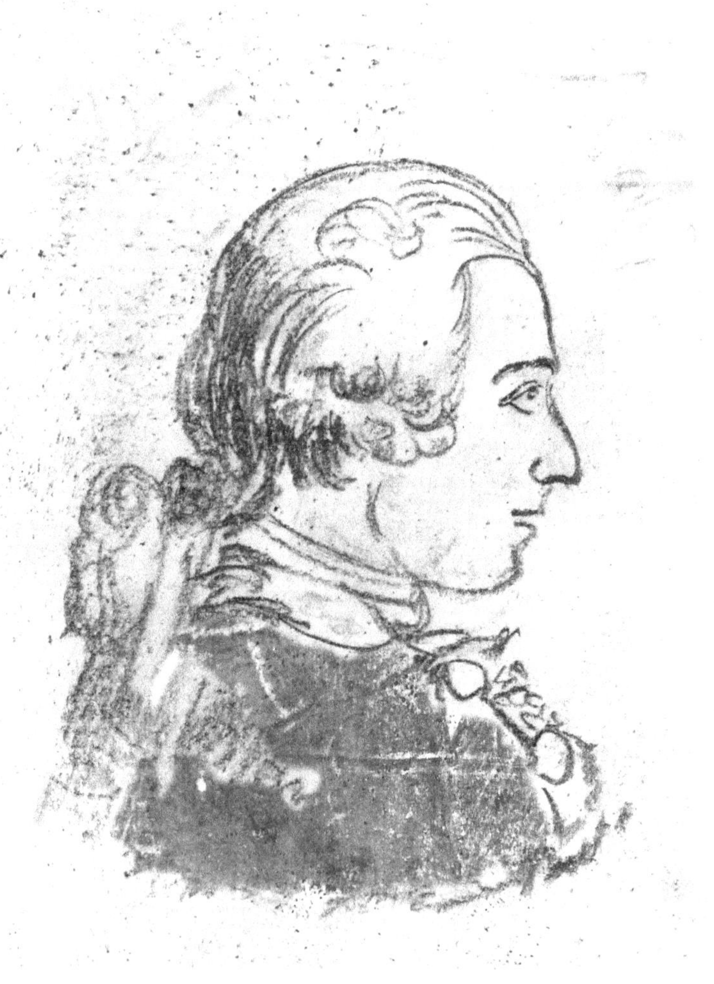

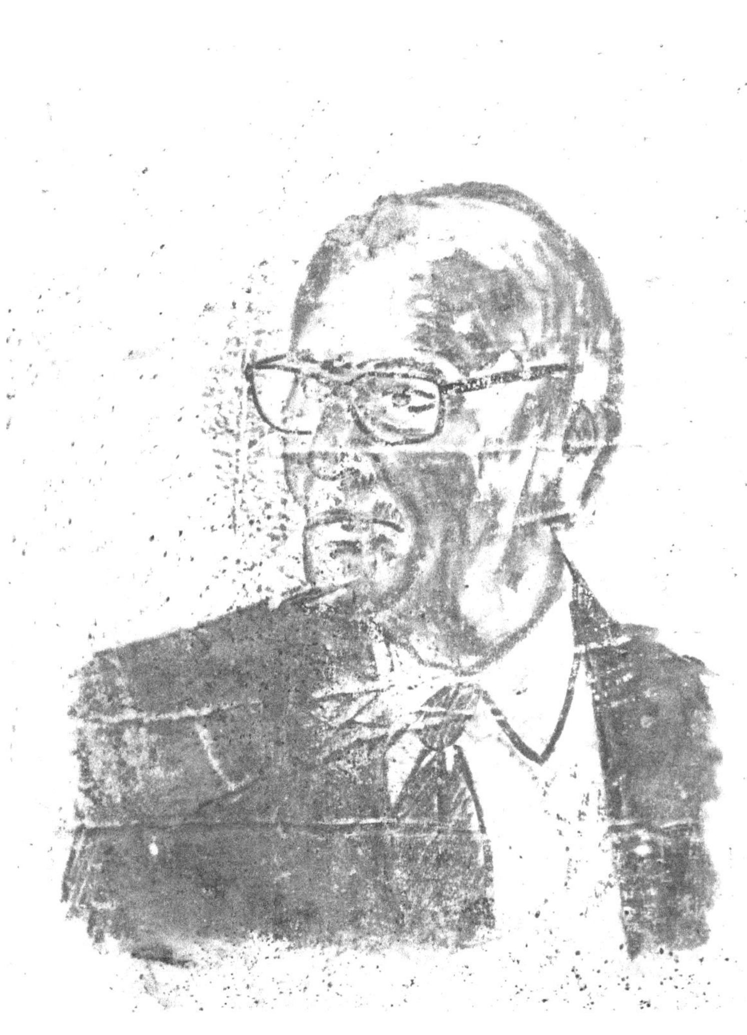

The scene: Pierre Cardin is enjoying an afternoon aperitif in his private study in the ruined but partially-restored Chateau de Lacoste when his housekeeper knocks on the door to announce a visitor.

Housekeeper: He says he is the Marquis de Sade.

Cardin: Very imaginative. Show him in.

[A dour-faced man long past his prime enters the room. Leaning heavily on a walking stick, he extends a well-stockinged leg and bows to Cardin.]

Sade: Good day to you, sir. I am Donatien Alphonse François, known more commonly by my title, the Marquis de Sade. You may call me simply "D" so as not to fall into the error often committed by the *hoi polloi*, who think my given name is "Marc," like the ill-fated Roman general, and my sur name is "Sade," which they mispronounce so it serves as the root of "sadism," the only thing their tiny brains can associate with me. As you know, once passion is gone, humanity is left with nothing but its detritus. I object to that stain on my reputation, which is the reason for my visit.

Cardin: Please, elucidate.

Sade: Very well. You, sir, I am sure, have a deeper understanding of my life's work than most. You realize, I hope, that I am not a monster, not a Caligula or Nero, but rather an artist—a performance artist, to apply a more precise label. The passion for destruction is a creative passion. The courage to imagine the otherwise is our greatest resource, adding color and suspense to all our life.

Cardin: I will grant such for this discussion.

Sade: Your reply belies your real feelings on the subject, my friend, but no matter. My art served its purpose: to awaken, to release, to confront the psyche of the audience. Note, if you will that art requires an audience.

Without someone to see it, hear it, read it, feel it, smell it perhaps, the work is not art. It is self-gratification.

Cardin: I am surprised! You object to self-gratification?

Sade: Of course not. There is nothing wrong with the practice in its many forms. But let us not conflate art performed in public with acts of masturbation created for private entertainment.

[Both men chuckle]

I see you've built a theater and dedicated it to performances on behalf of various public benefit organizations. I suppose that's quite laudable, but may I inquire as to your real reasons?

Cardin: I prefer to not explore that subject. I would rather ask why you built a theater on these grounds yourself. Was it to provide a modicum of culture to the villagers? Or for your own amusements?

Sade: I can assure you I had no intention of entertaining the cretins who deliver my groceries and clean the shit out of my stables. They were not my audience. The theater was for the full expression of my art to edify a very select group consisting of myself and my dearest associates. It provided a less restrictive venue than the bed chamber for my little performance pieces about the many facets of passion. Besides, telling my actors and actresses they would be appearing on stage made them much more receptive to my creative concepts.

Cardin: Very clever! [He pauses to consider the possibilities.]

So you believe your indulgent journeys along the borders of sexual depravity to be a form of art?

Sade: But of course! Don't you? What else would they be? After all, as I said before, what is true art—not the commercial pablum we see in the museums and galleries—other than the expression of the artist's innermost feeling about his very existence? Such expressions can take many forms, as you well know. I chose to act out tableau that reflected the conclusions I have drawn about the human race and my position above it. That is art. You do the same, do you not?

Cardin: I beg your pardon! How can you equate my work with the horrors you present? I concede that both may be art as you define the term, but my entire career has been devoted to beauty, not pain and degradation. To expressing my love for women by presenting their glorious bodies in new and delightful ways.

Sade: Ha! Ha! Ha! Delightful to whom? How does a mini-skirt feel to the woman whose genitals are barely covered? Does such titillating exposure enhance her self-worth? Or does it express your own lewd desires to be teased by glimpses of her buttocks?

Cardin: No one ever said art must be pleasant in the conventional sense to either the audience or the artist—and certainly not to the model. Art must evoke feeling, however, or the artist has produced nothing more than wallpaper or elevator music.

Sade: Curiosity about life in all of its aspects, I think, is still the secret of great creative people. And so we come to agreement. Also to the final reason for my visit.

Cardin: Which is?

Sade: I want to thank you for collaborating with Alexander Burganov to present my likeness in such a unique form to express the essence of my creative life. My head in a cage! How reflective of the public opinion that turned my name into something nasty. We must always beware of the unfortunate classified as virtuous. The cage certainly reminds the viewer that I spent thirty years in prison creating my works. Were those works of fiction or of fact? Ah, the enigma of my crossed arms in the monument show that I will never tell. The reality of my art blooms in its only true venue—within the mind of the reader.

Cardin: So true, so true. May I offer you a libation?

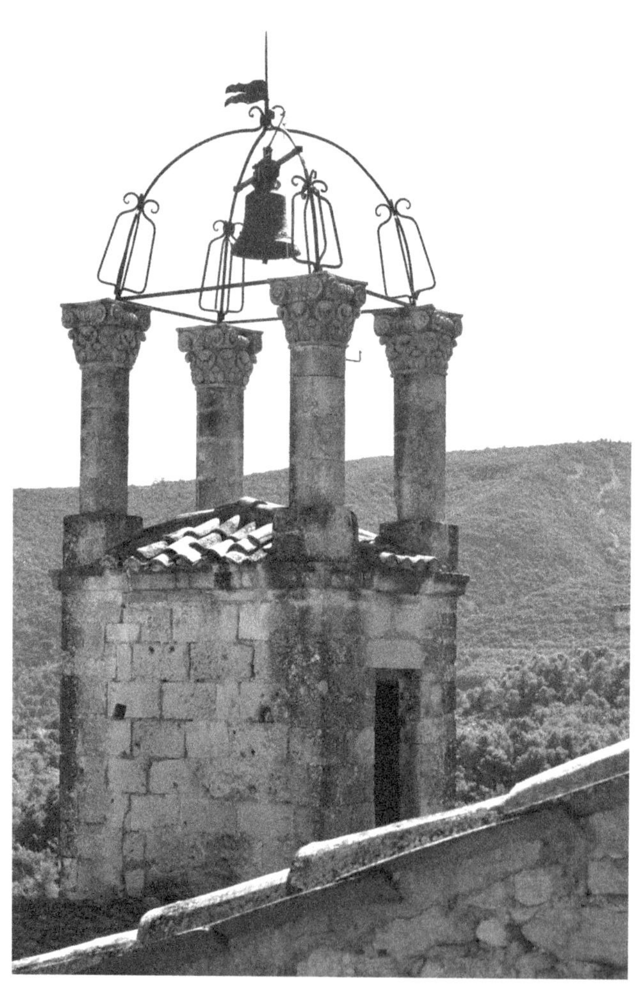

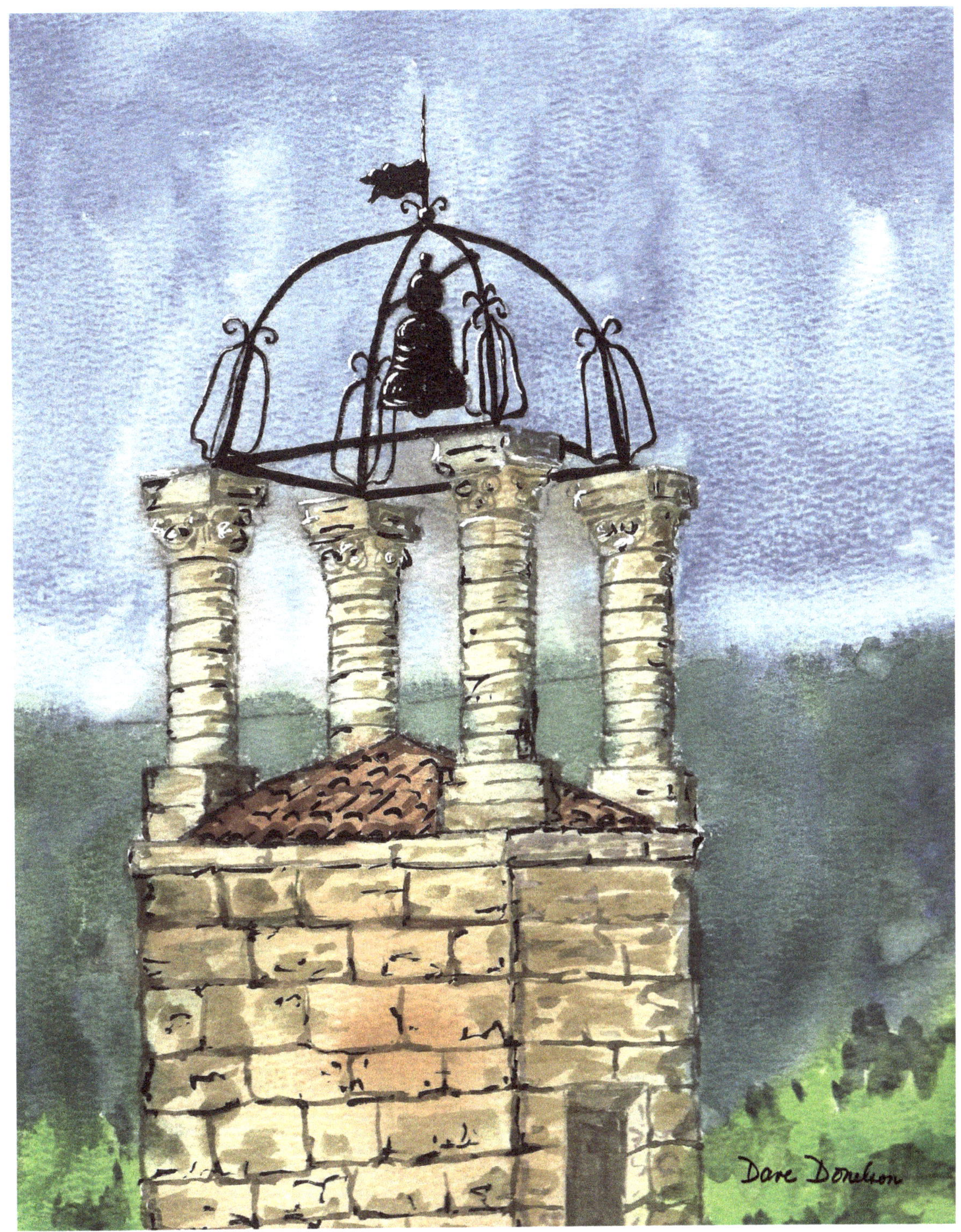

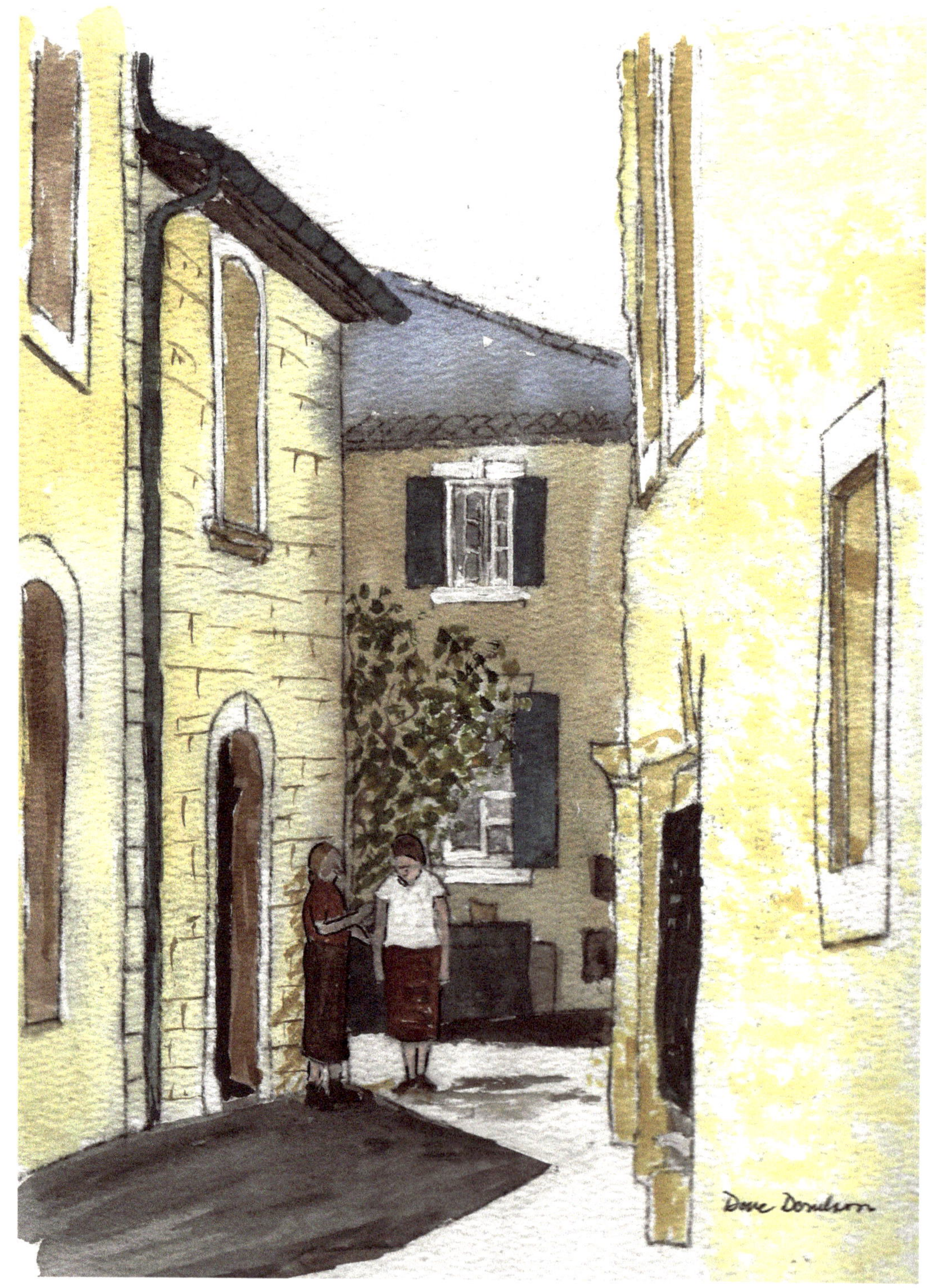
Dave Donelson

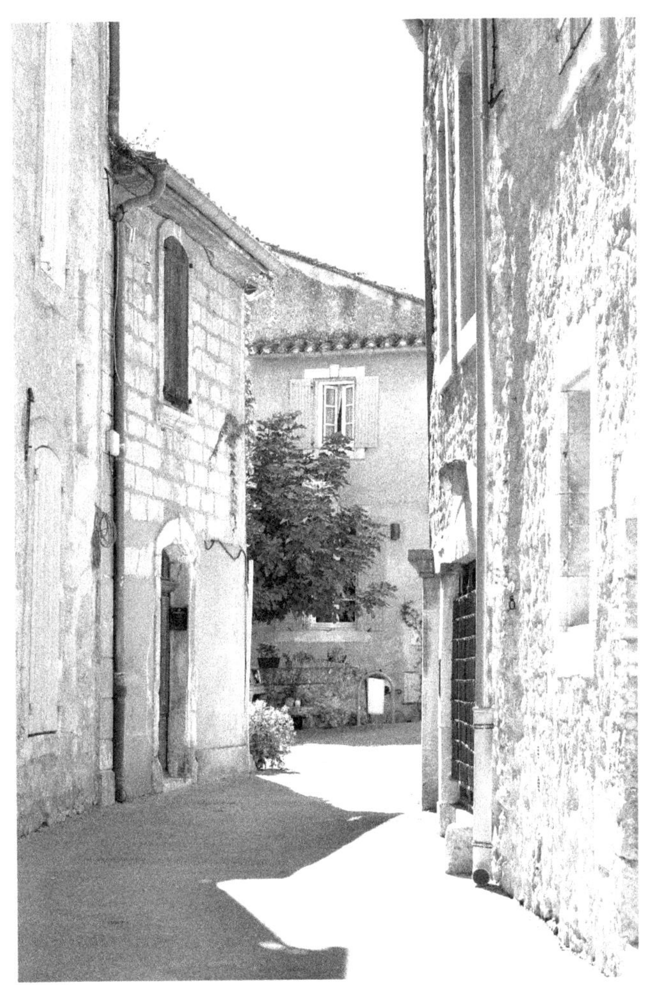

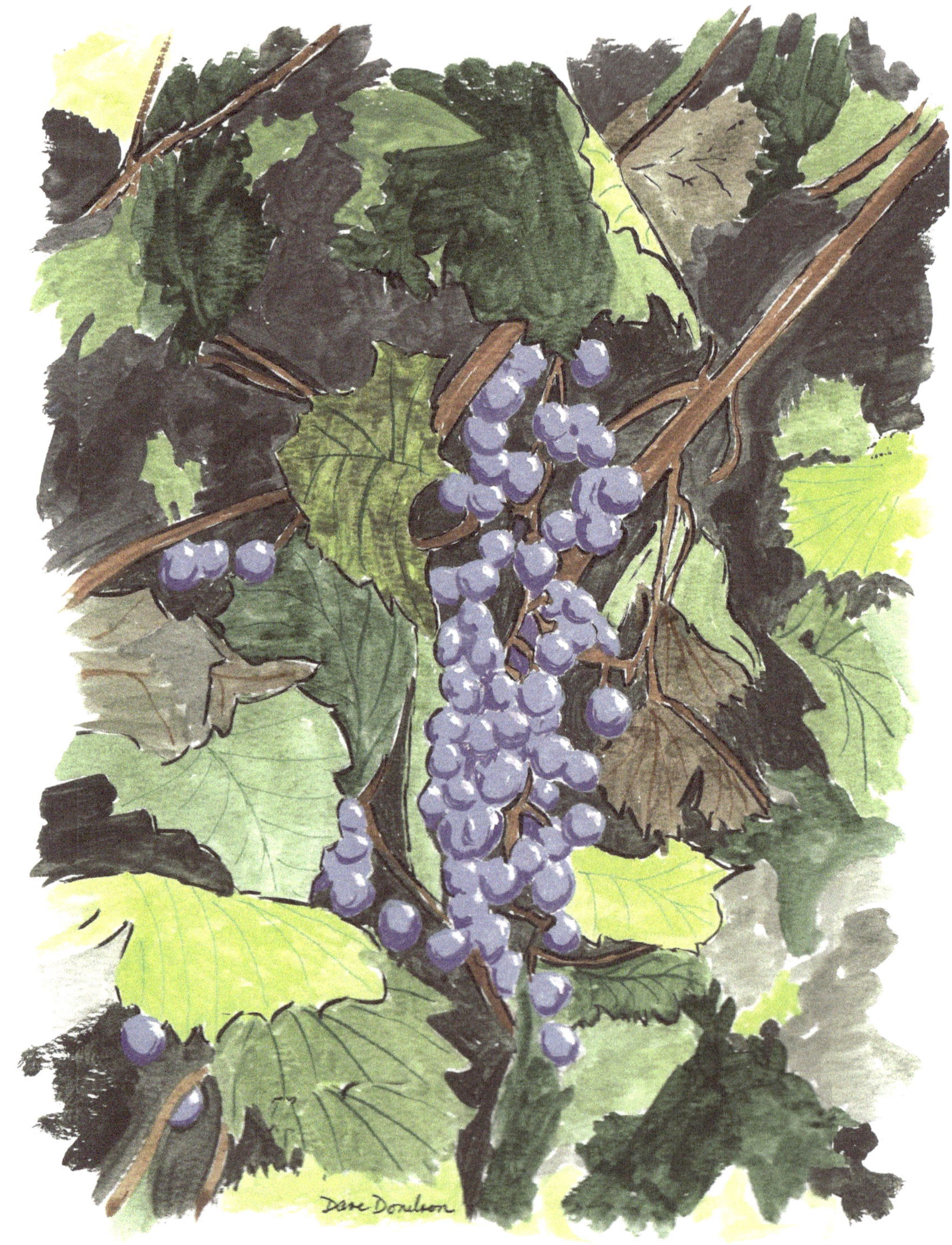
Dave Donelson

Chapter Four

Community of Art

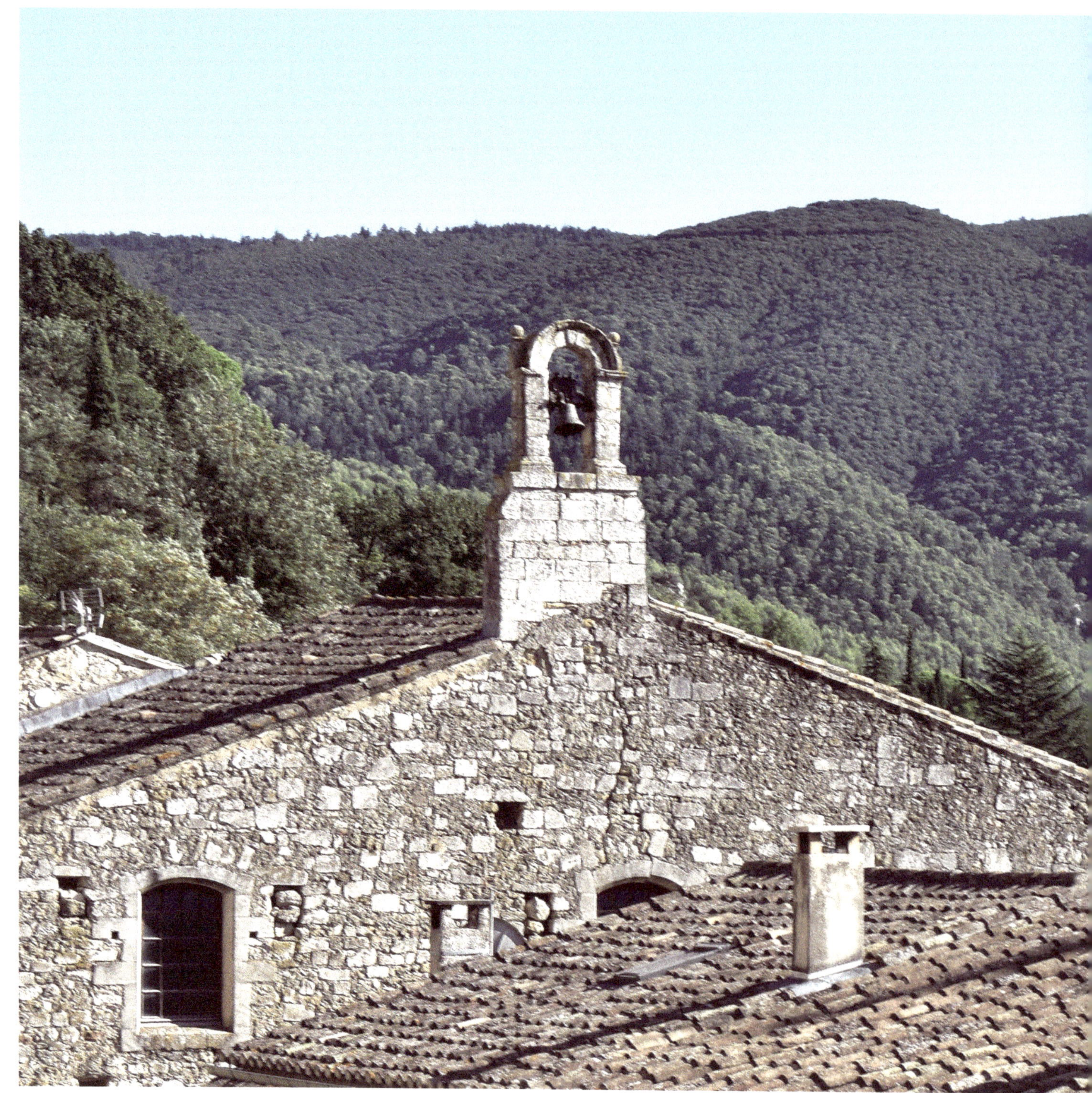

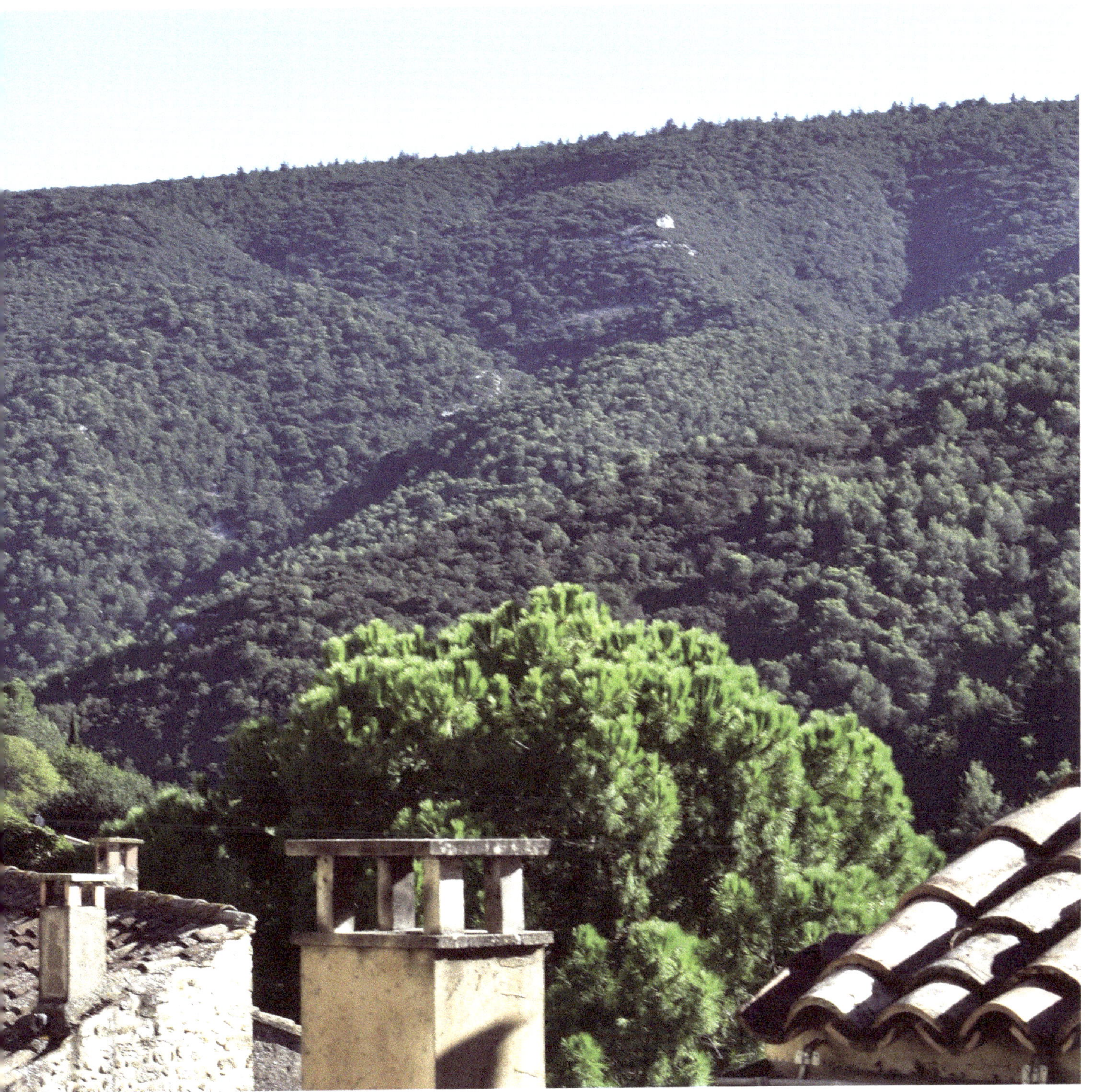

Gordes

Gorges is where artists live, create, and show their work. Its brilliant buildings shining in tiers from the valley to the mountain top has drawn them since World War II when Marc Chagall fled to the village to escape the Germans in Paris. He moved his family and studio into an old mill in the Fontaine Basse area of the village, a district in the hollow of the valley on an esplanade where water from springs that pass under the cliff powered mills as early as the 15th century.

"There, in the south of France, for the first time in my life," Chagall said, "I saw rich greenness the like of which I had never seen in my own country." It was in Gordes that Chagall worked on "The Madonna of the Village" and many other paintings. When the Vichy government began to intern Jews, he and his wife fled to America, where they stayed until after the war.

Many other artists found Gordes a welcoming, inspiring location for their studios, especially in the summer months. Among them were Victor Vasarely, considered the father of Op Art, who taught there and whose works were showcased in the Chateau de Gordes from 1970 to 1996. In addition to Vasarely, the Chateau housed a museum dedicated to Flemish painter Pol Mara from 1997 to 2011. The Chateau is a rectangular castle built in 1525 by Bertrand Rambaud de Simiane, the Baron de Gordes. Today it offers a variety of annual exhibitions.

Other artists associated with Gordes include Jean Deyrolle, a leader of the second generation of abstract artists, cubist Andre Lhote, Victor Spahn, contemporary painter of sports, and photographer Willy Ronis.

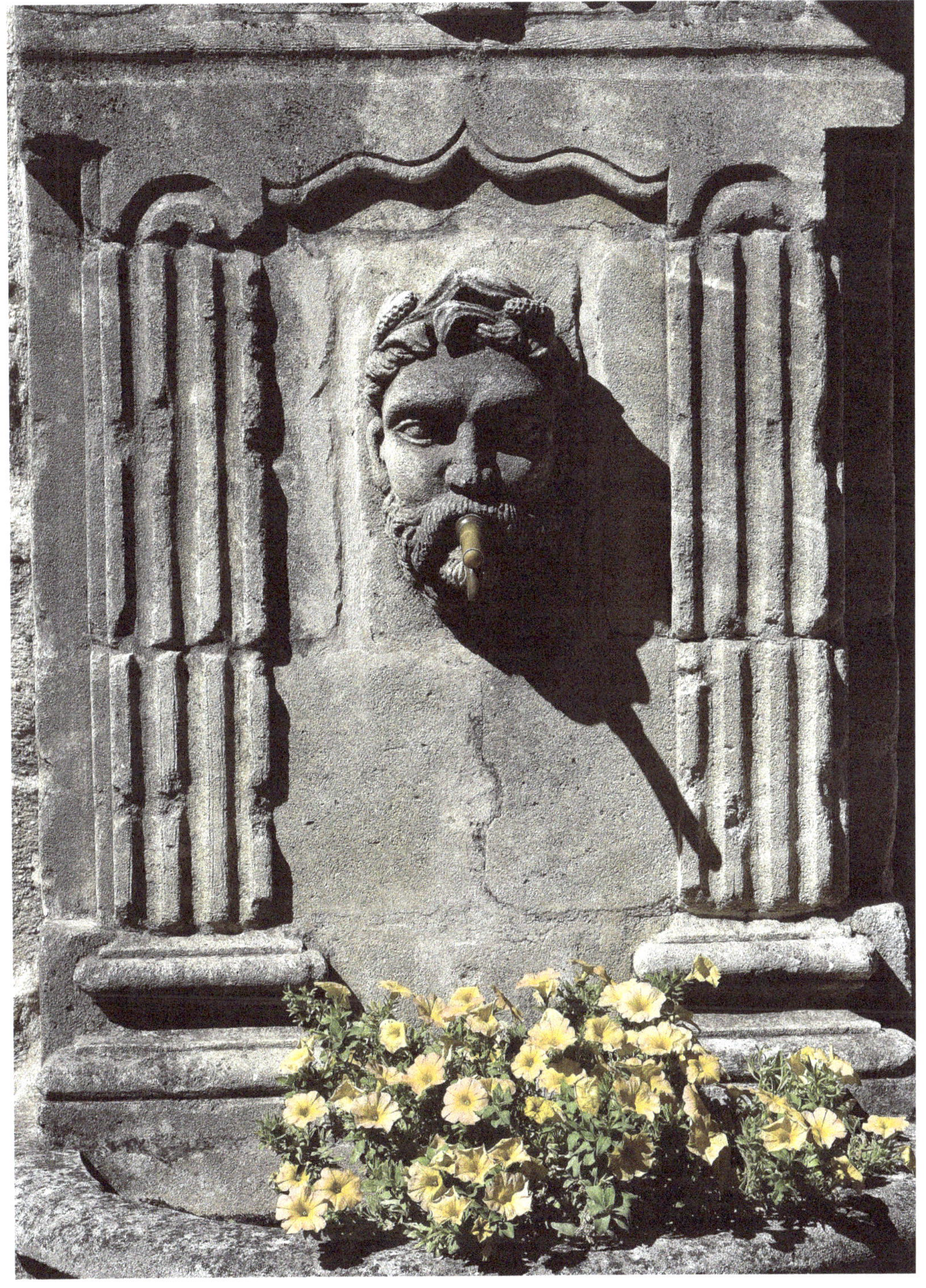

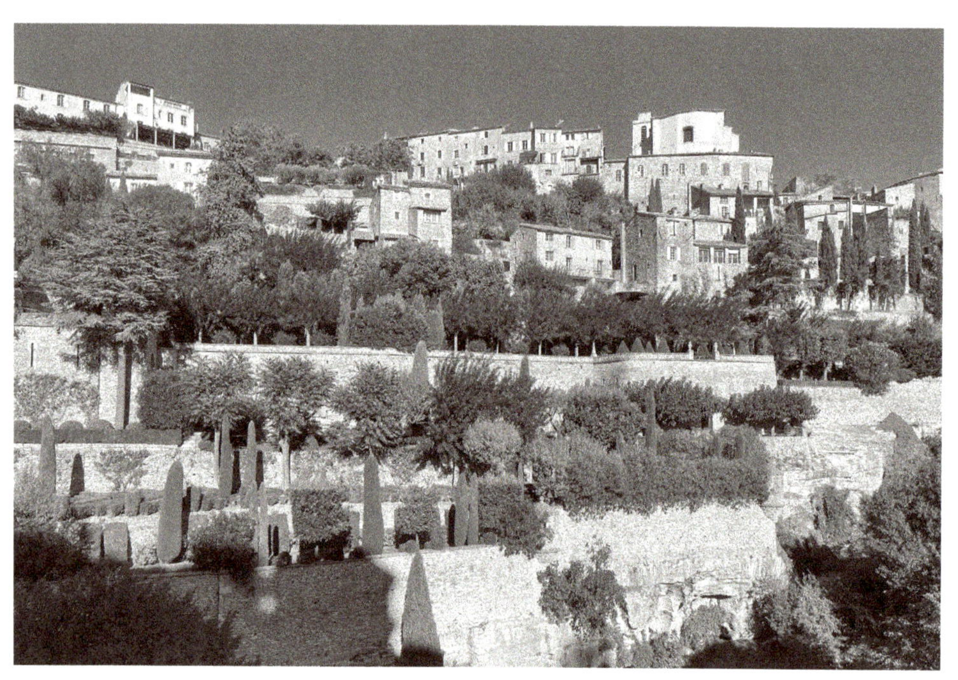

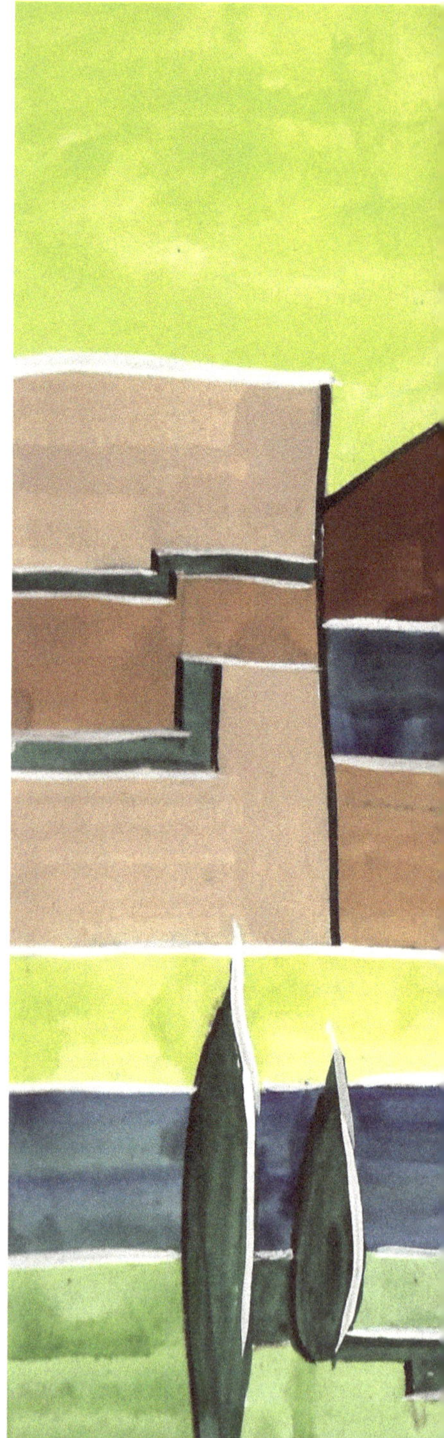

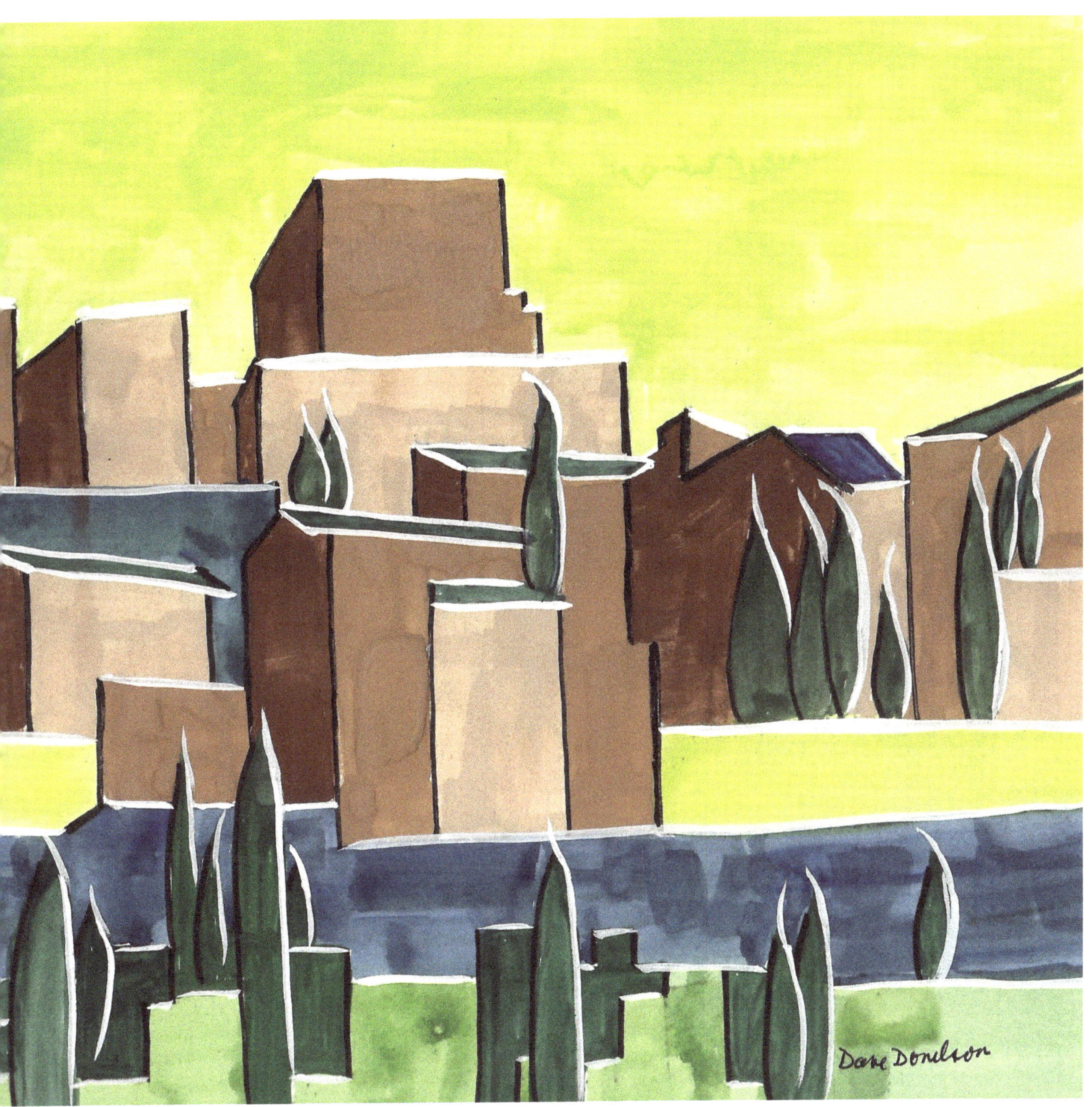
Dave Donelson

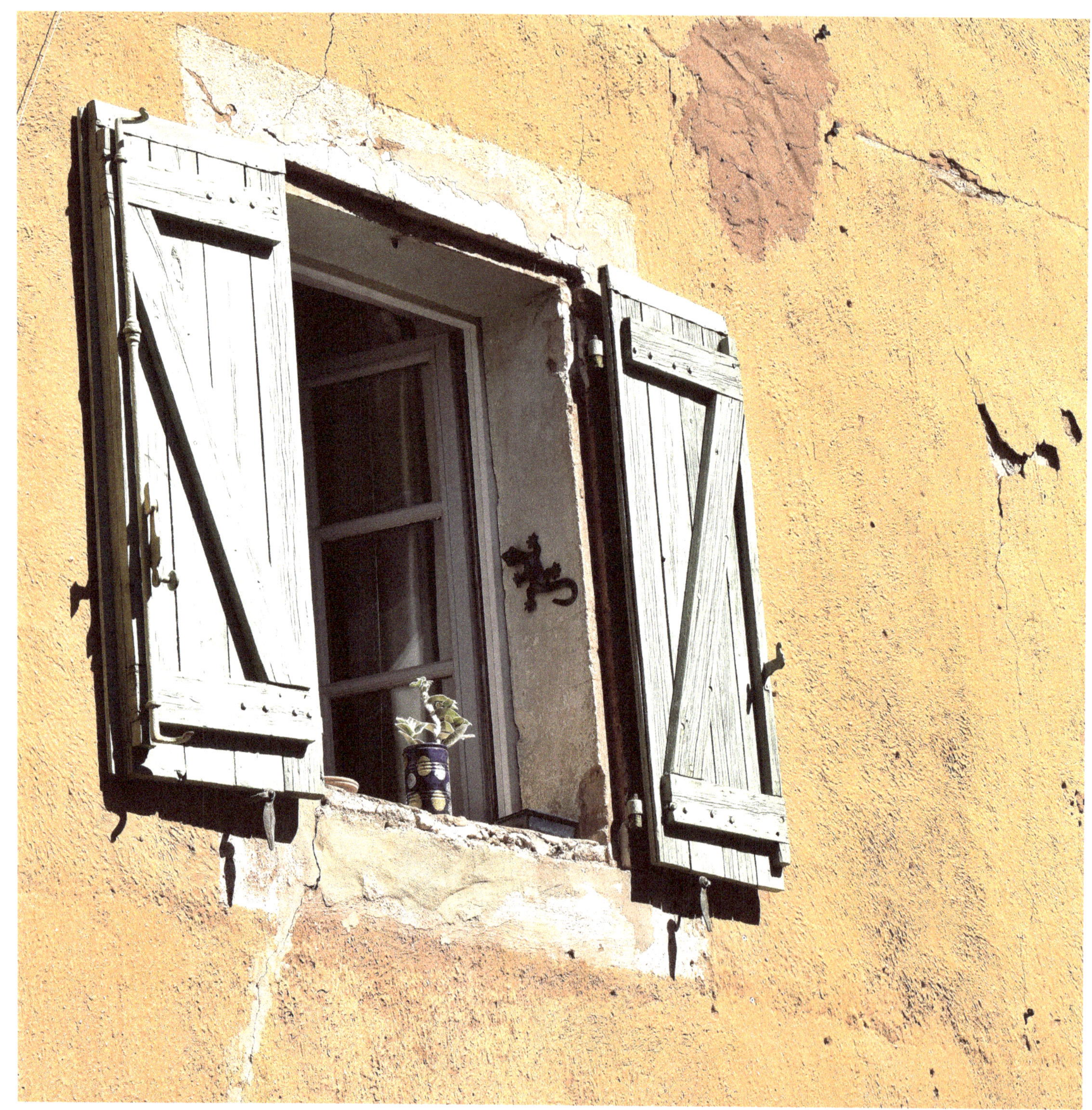

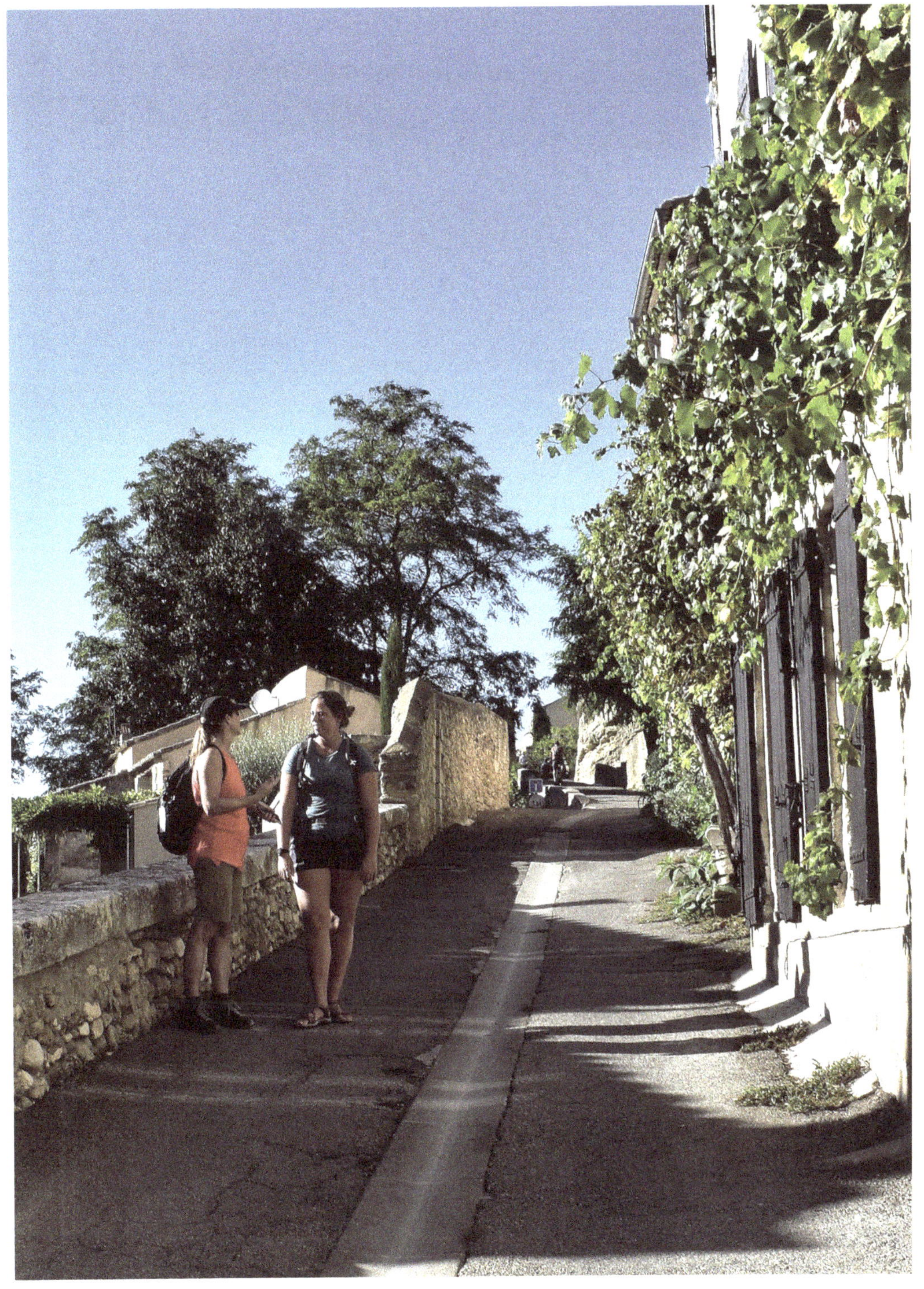

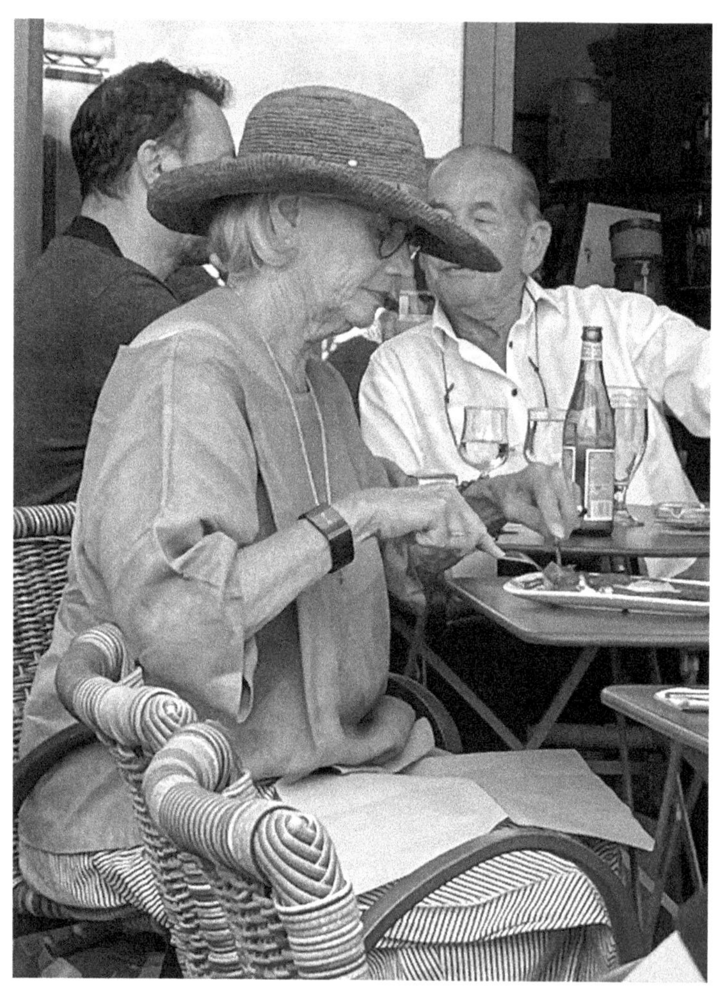

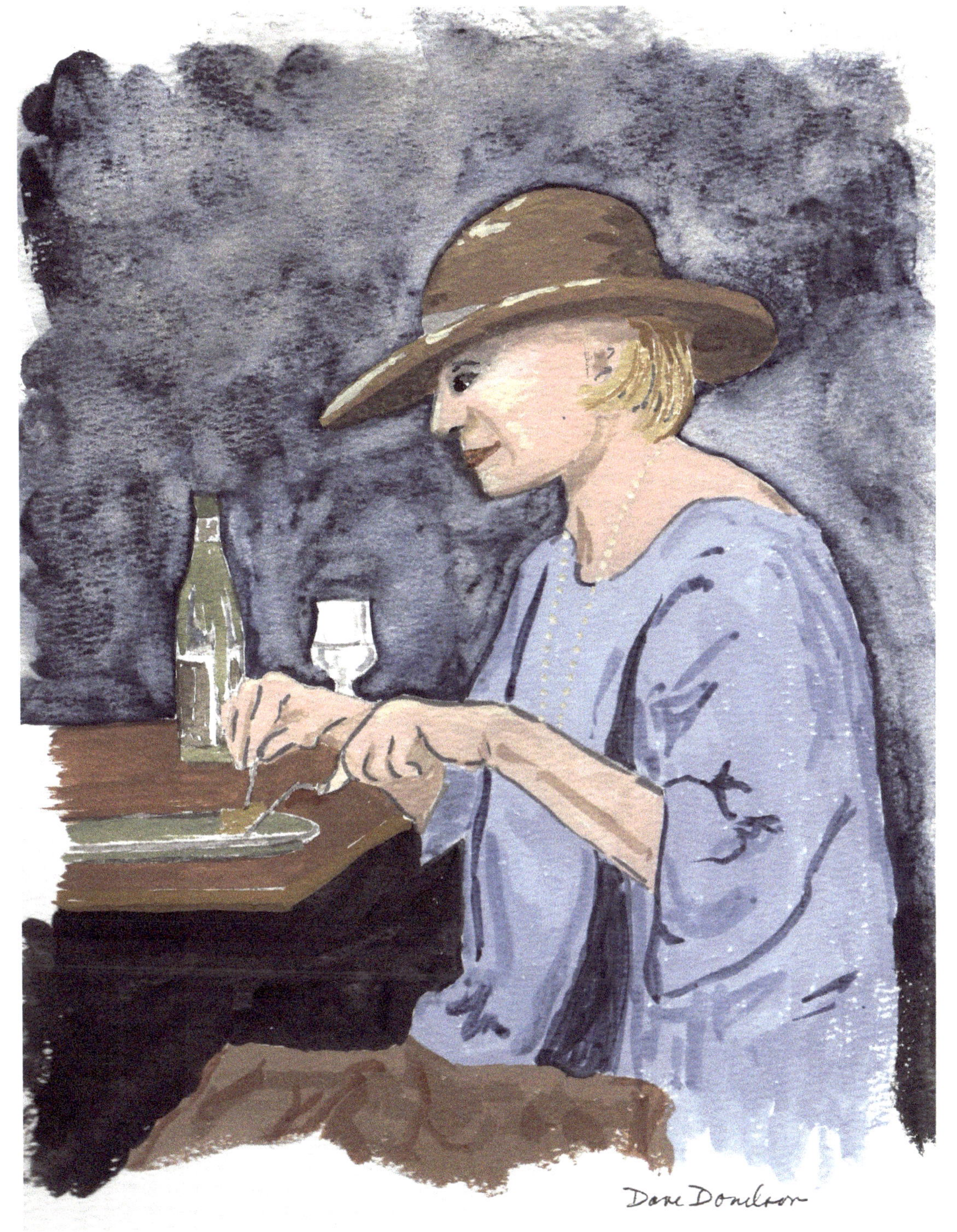

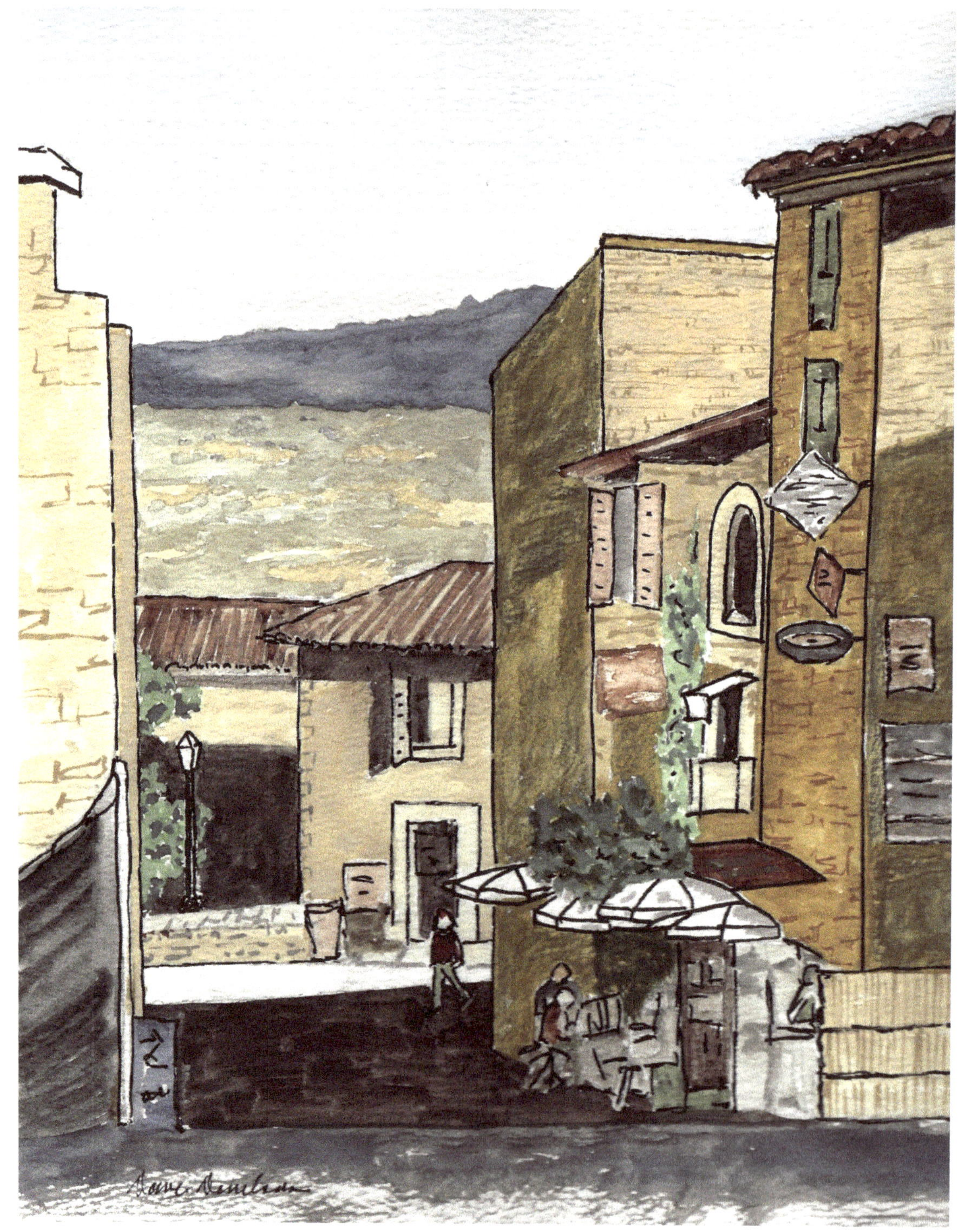

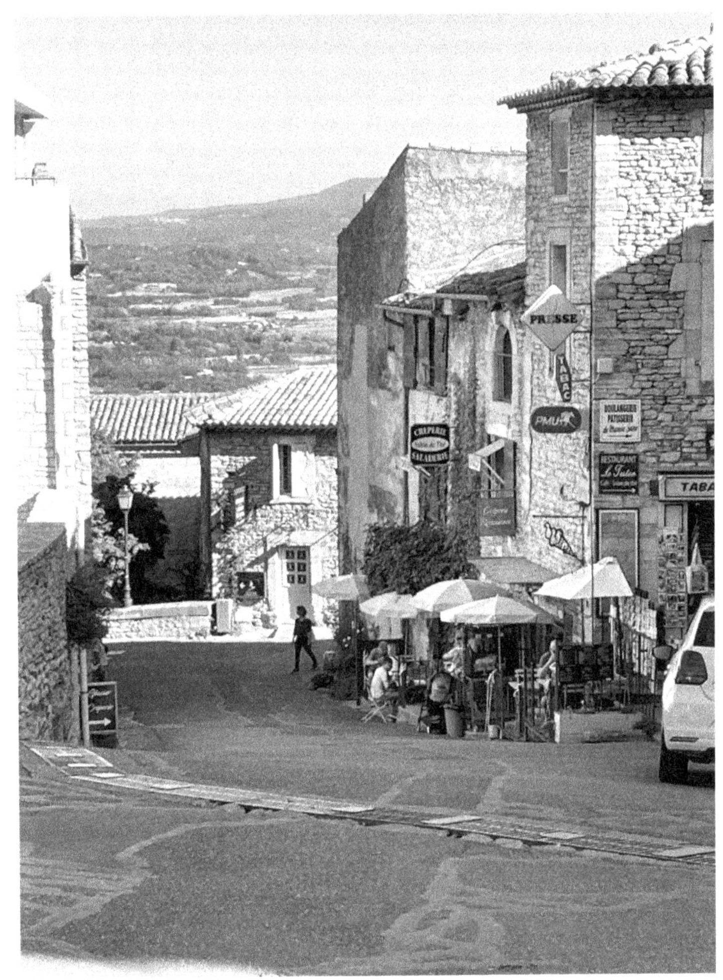
PRESSE
TABAC
PMU
BOULANGERIE
PATISSERIE
RESTAURANT
TABA

Lavandula

Lavender in it many varieties is endemic to Provence. In its naturally growing form, its flower was used by the Romans to perfume their baths and their clothes. By the middle ages, it was cultivated in monasteries alongside medicinal plants. As the perfume industry grew, Provence responded with beautiful natural fields, but it wasn't until the mid-20th Century that a cultivar suitable for harvesting by machines was developed to grow in the colorful rows we see today. The vast fields depicted in the tourist literature are a modern invention. YAWN. What a banal story! I prefer my version of the local legend:

Lavandula was a blue-eyed mountain nymph born in the Alpes de Haute Provence. As a child, Lavandula loved to paint pictures of the flowers of her mountain home, especially her namesake, the wild lavender. She grew up to become a fine artist and a beautiful but restless maiden. One day, curious about the world, she came down from the mountain to see the valley below.

She found a scene she thought to paint, but as she leafed through her sketchbook to find a blank page, she came to a painting of her beloved mountain flowers. Their lush rich blues so outshone the dry, sere land of the plain in front of her that she began to cry.

Her tears fell on the paper in such profusion that the paint began to soften and finally to run and drip off the page. Seizing the wonderful opportunity, Lavandula kissed the wet blue paint with her soft carmine lips. Soon a puddle of violet tears gathered on the page. With a smile, she whirled around and around, holding her sketchbook open to scatter the colorful tears even further across the valley.

Lavandula soon returned to the mountains, having seen enough of the world to quell her wanderlust. The next spring, her tear-blessed lavender covered the valley.

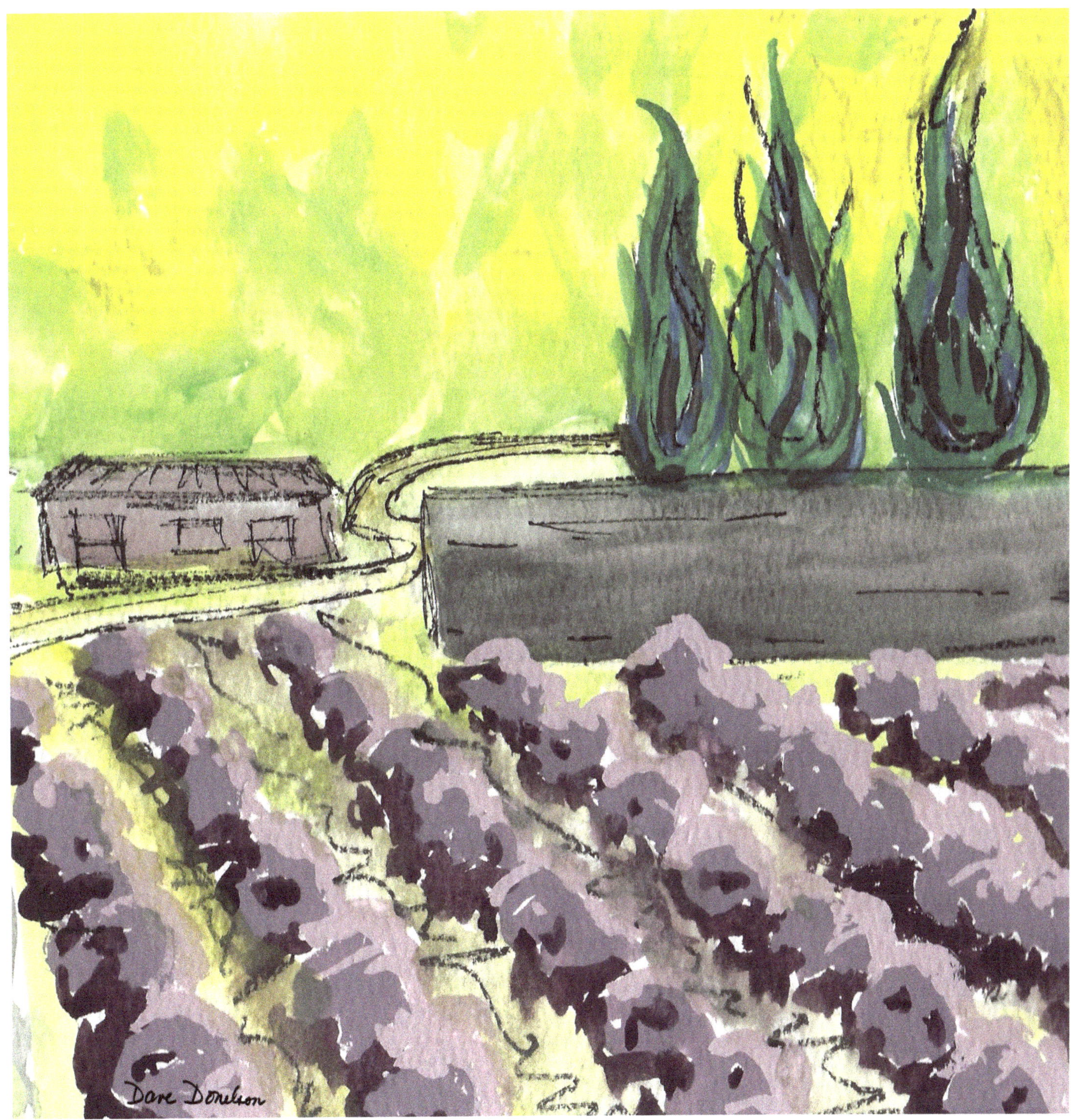
Dave Donelson

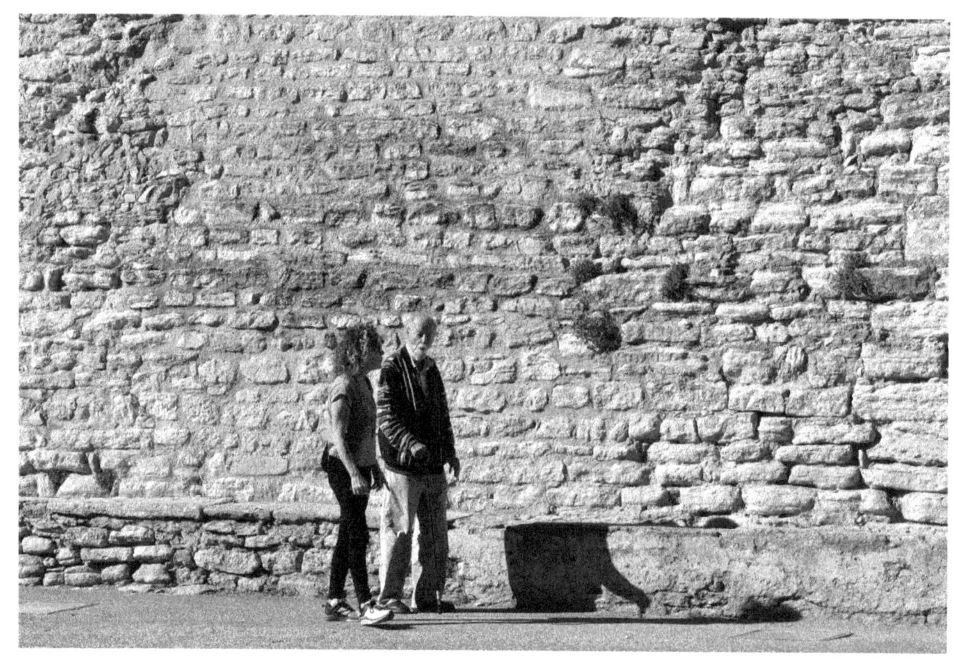

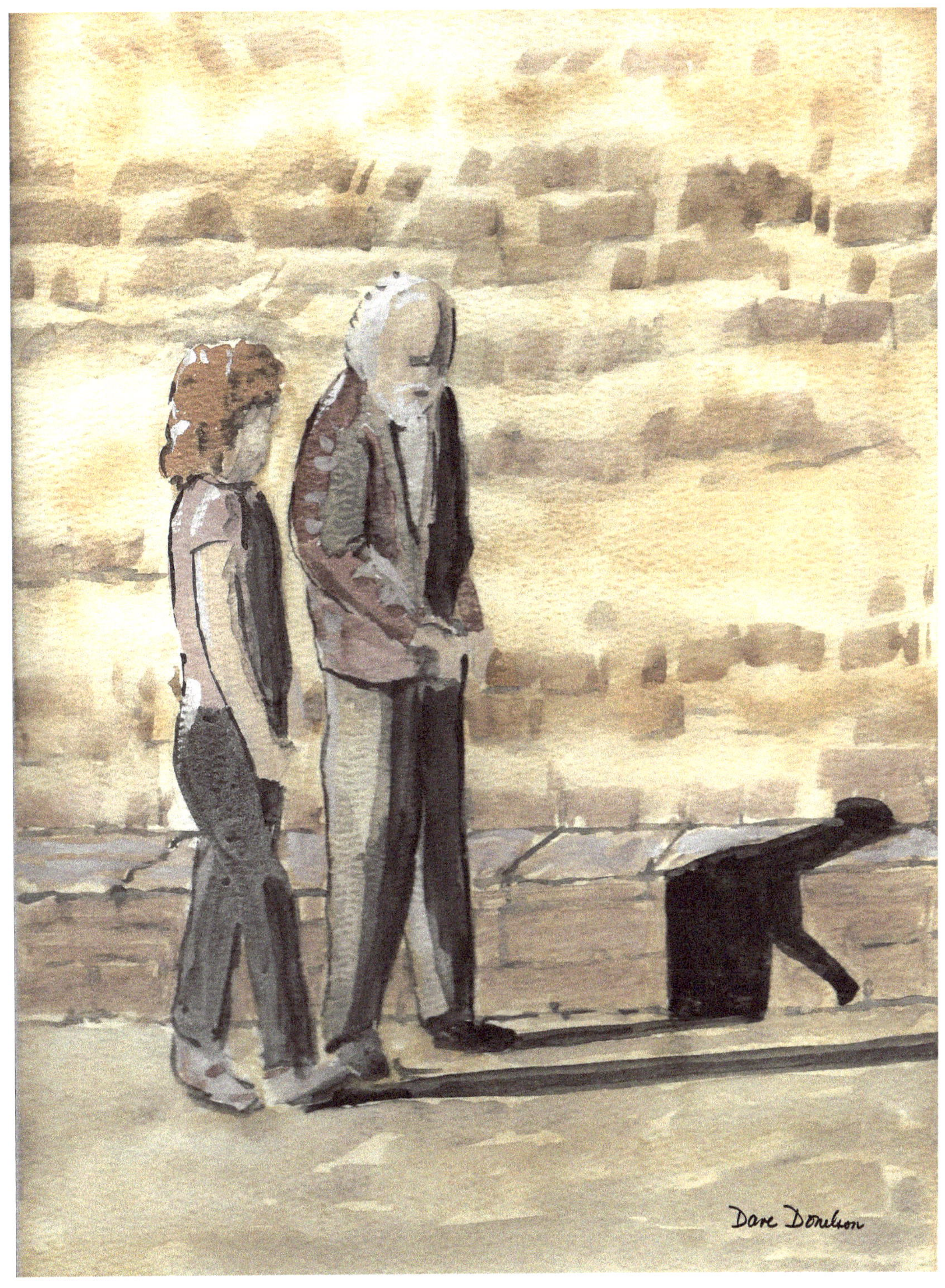
Dave Donelson

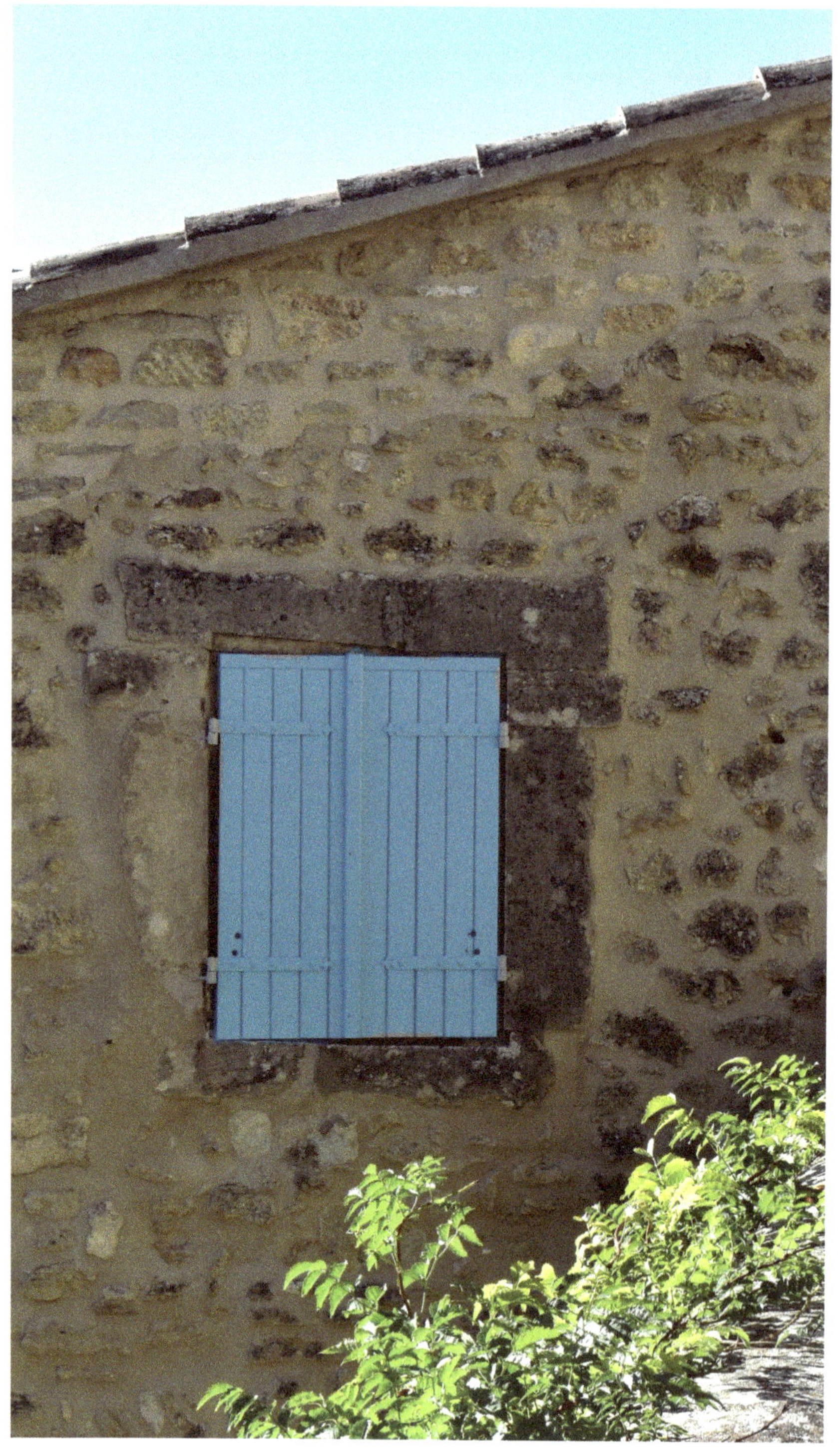

Chapter Five

High Ground

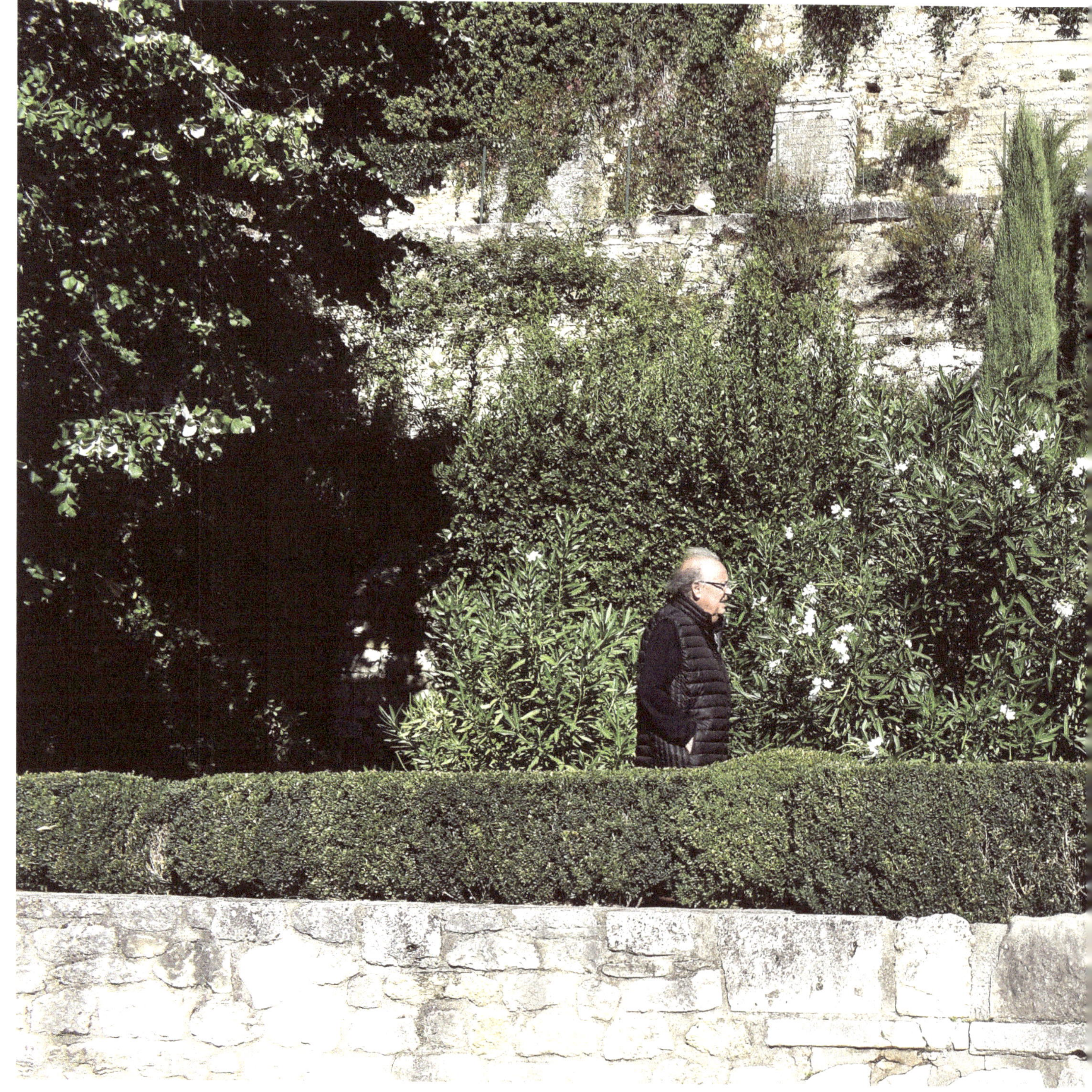

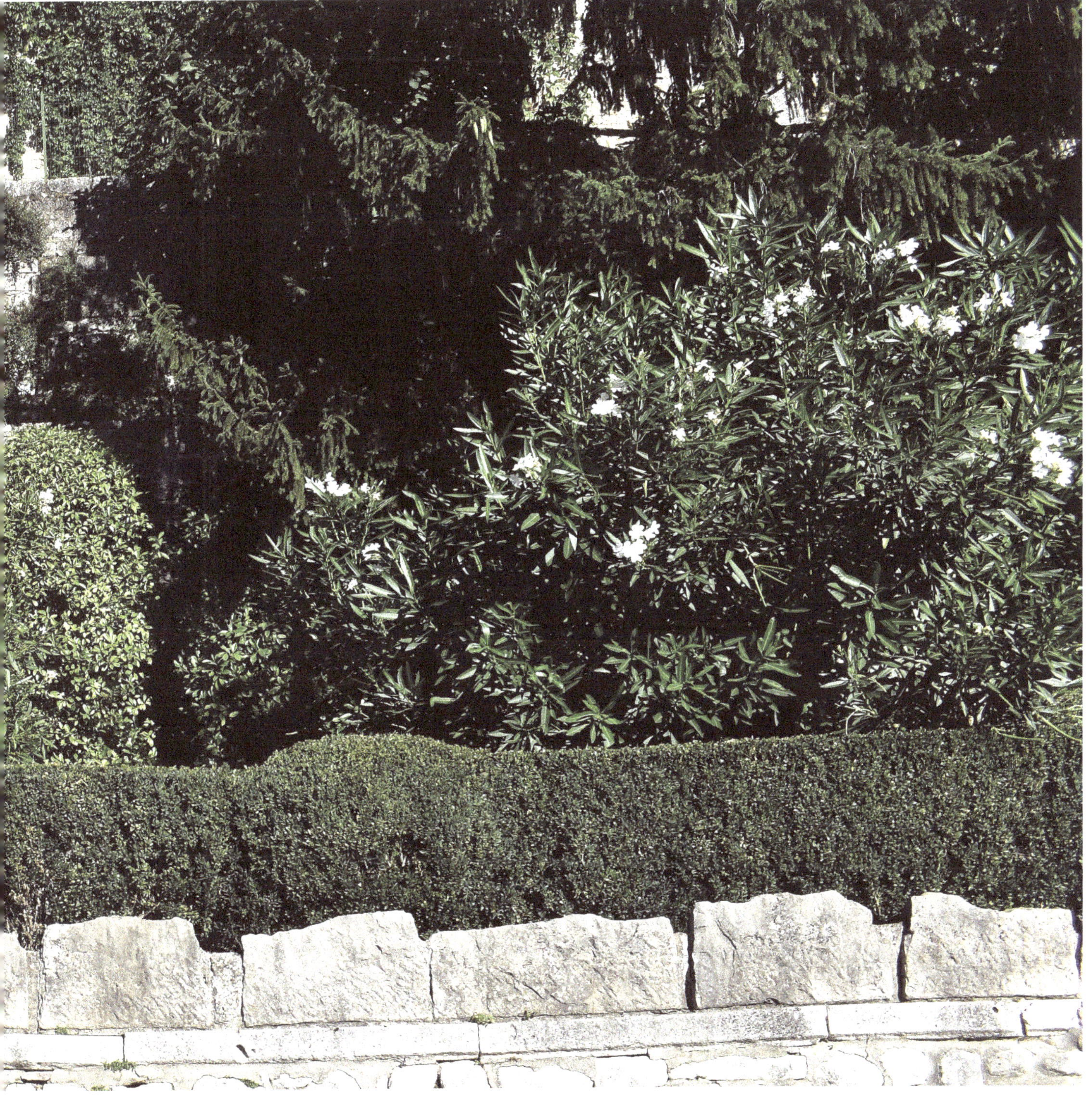

Menerbes

Everybody loves Menerbes. In fact, many have loved it so much they were willing to die to occupy it and control the land in the valley below. That probably includes the first known inhabitants, who lived in rock shelters near the present village some 35,000 years ago. Many centuries later, the area was invaded by the Vulgientes and Vordenses from Central Europe, then the Ligures, and eventually the Greeks and Romans. During the Middle Ages, they were replaced by the Germans, the Alans, the Vandals and the Ostrogoths. With such a history of invasion and occupation, it's not surprising that a fortified village was eventually constructed. One of the principal structures was Le Castelet, literally a small castle that still exists today, probably built some hundred years or so after the black plague decimated the region's population in 1348.

Fortifications like Le Castelet are all about control. When you occupy the high ground, you command the surrounding countryside. Your high vantage point gives you a better view of your enemies and their activities, allowing you to swoop down and attack them, then retire to the safety of the high ground you own. Your arrows and cannon balls fly farther because they're spinning downward with the assistance of gravity, whereas your attackers' projectiles are weakened by traveling in the opposite direction. Once established on the highest point, you are very difficult to dislodge. This is especially true if you build yourself a stone fort on top of the hill. Or if you construct a church there.

Because religion, too, is all about control. Men (almost never women) claim they were appointed by God to tell you how to live, what to do, what not to do, and when to do or not do it. If you believe them, or even if you don't believe them but fear them, you will give them a significant portion of your assets, your labor, and perhaps your life. You will build forts and/or churches for them. You will fight and die for them. They tell you that you will be rewarded for your loyalty in the afterlife. Know, though, that you will be punished, often quite severely, for disloyalty or disobedience while you are still alive.

Power, pure and simple.

You can substitute "politics" for "religion" in the preceding paragraph, although few modern politicians claim to rule by virtue of divine appointment, at least in the United States (with some notable exceptions). Throughout human history, politics and religion have been allies and/or enemies in their pursuit of control. It would be difficult to find a better example of their intermarriage than the events that led to the infamous siege of Menerbes.

In the early 16th century, the region became a hotbed of Protestantism, prompting the Vatican and French authorities to team up to persecute and massacre the "heretics" who lived there during the wars of religion that decimated the entire country. The 1572 St. Bartholomew's Day massacre in Paris sparked Protestant leaders to seize Le Castelet with 150 armed men the following year. Within days, Catholic armies from as far away as Corsica surrounded Menerbes with an army that eventually grew to 15,000 men and laid a siege that lasted five years. During countless assaults, Le Castelet received over 900 cannon shots causing numerous fires and much destruction. Eventually, the 120 survivors surrendered and were allowed to return to their homes. The Catholics retained their political control of the region and the country.

Some portions of the original Castellet remain, although large scale renovations done in the 19th century concealed much of its design. It is today a private home. One modern-era owner of Le Castellet was Nicolas de Stael, a Russian-born painter, who bought it in 1953, produced 254 paintings in the next fifteen months, but died by his own hand in Antibes in 1955.

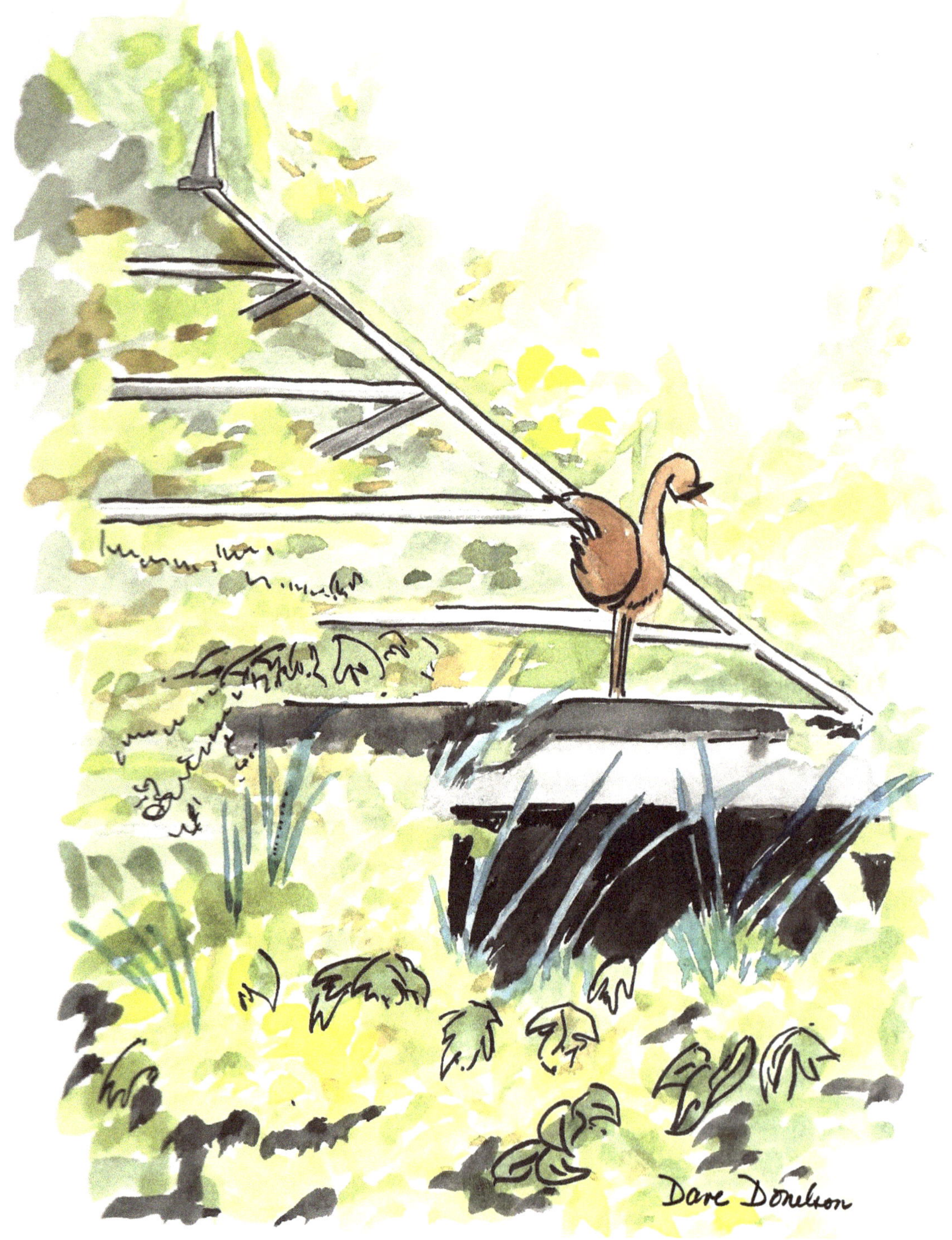
Dave Donelson

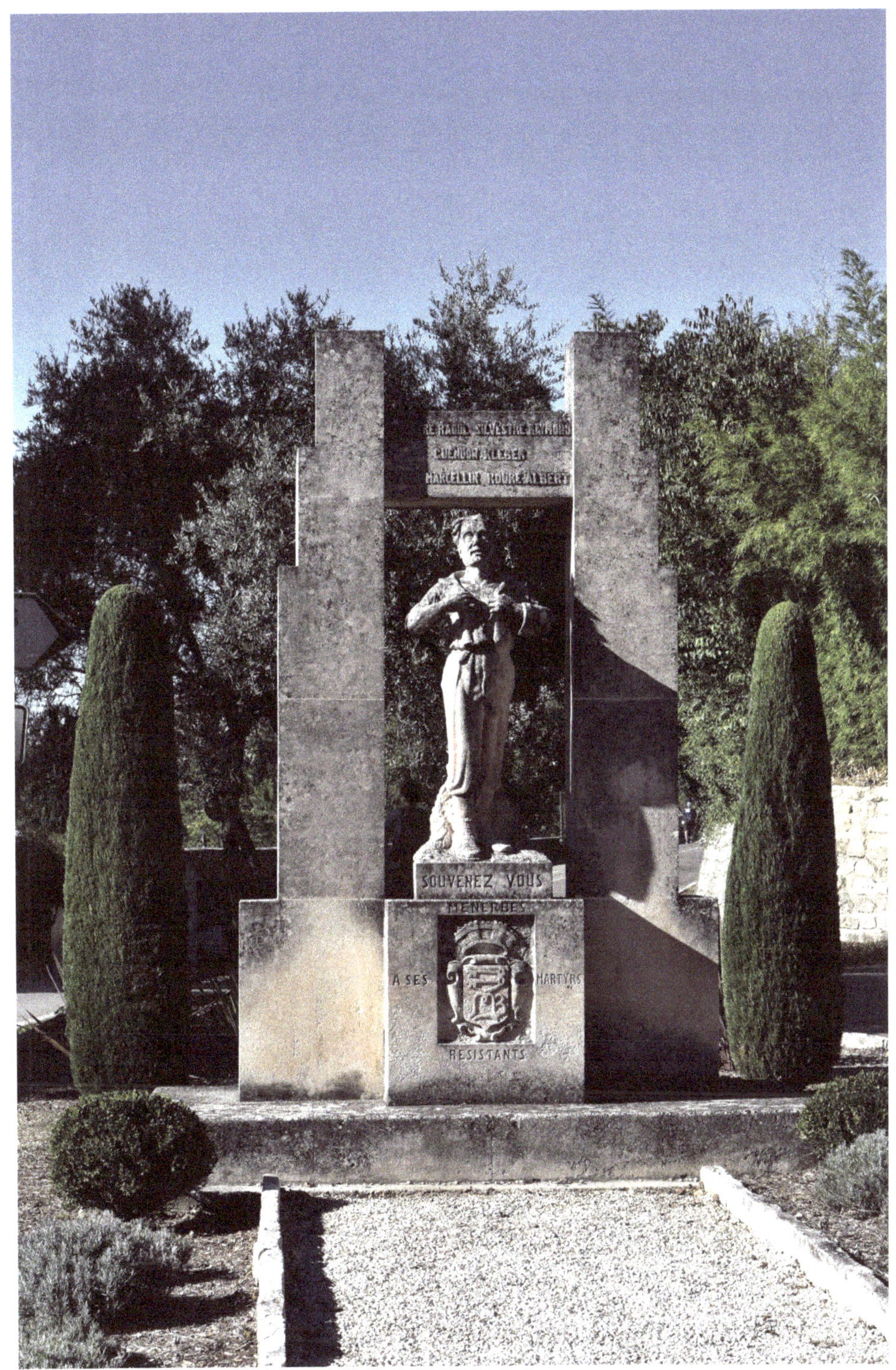
MARCELLIN ROURE ALBERT
SOUVENEZ VOUS
MENERBES
A SES
MARTYRS
RESISTANTS

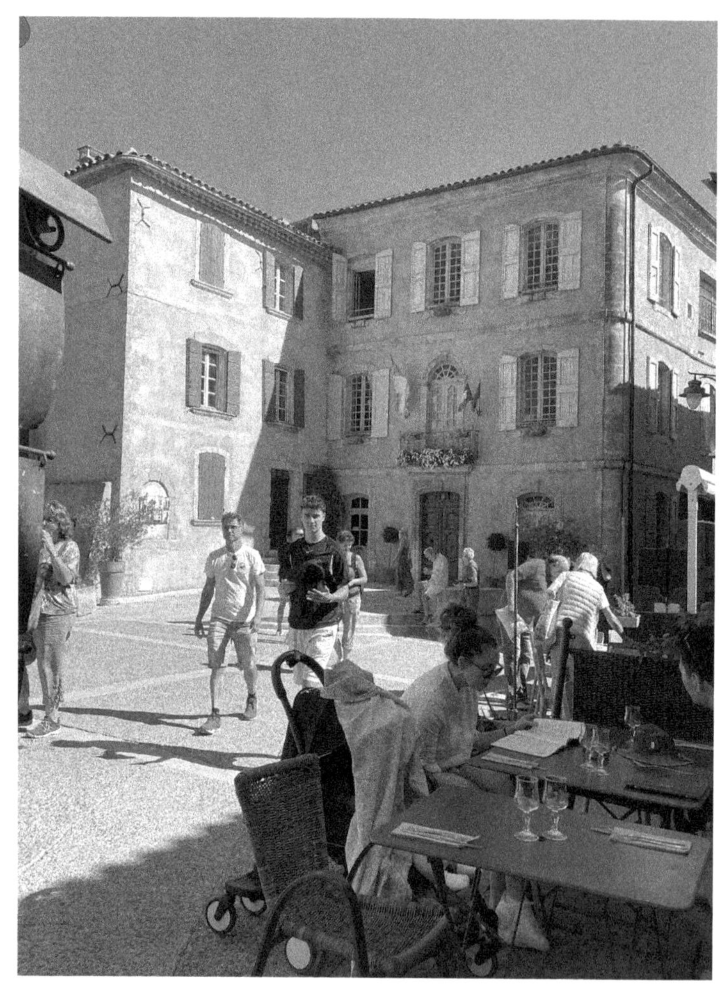

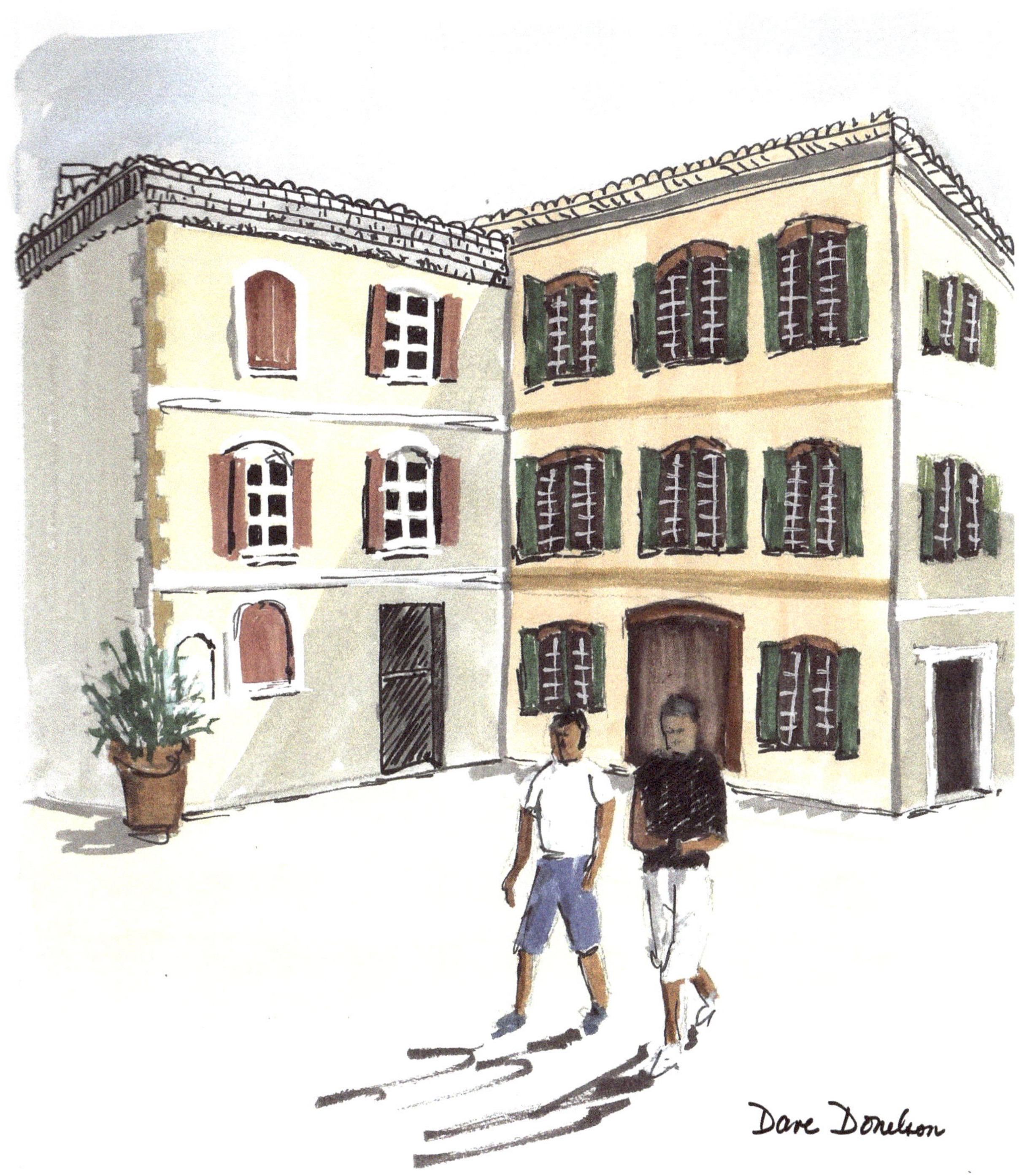
Dave Donelson

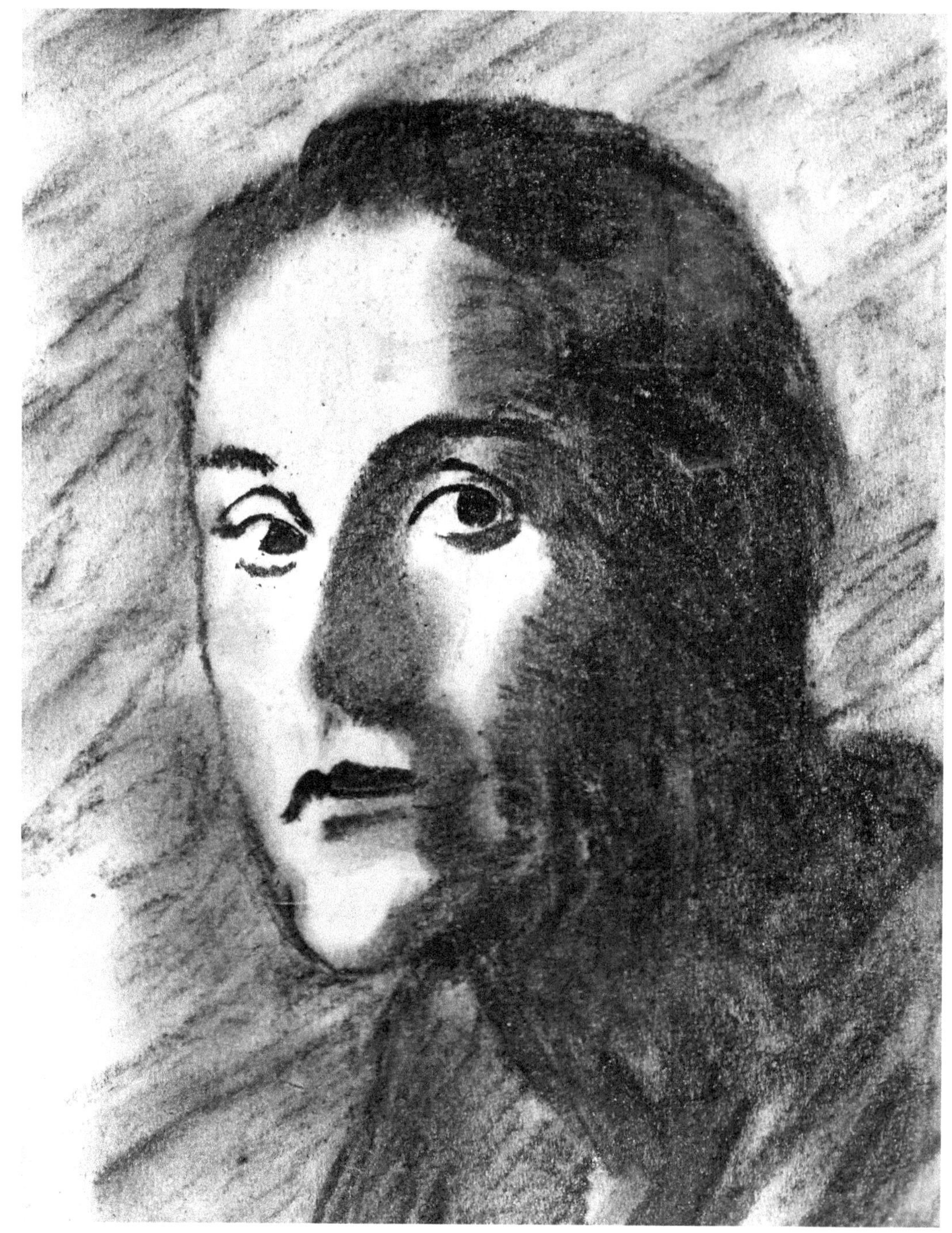

Soliloquy of Dora Maar

He painted me endlessly, but never well. Yes, I was "The Weeping Woman," but all his portraits of me are lies, they're all Picasso. Not one is Dora Maar.

Pablo told me he was giving me the house in Menerbes with a wave of his hand as if he were dismissing a filthy beggar. When I knew he was leaving, my day turned into night. He went back to Paris where we met. I followed my anger here in the south into deep black despair.

He went to yet someone else. Someone younger. Someone less a threat to him than I. For I was a surrealist photographer as well -known in my world as Pablo was in his when we met. My work was displayed at one time alongside that of Man Ray and Salvador Dali. Pablo never forgave me my fame. He said that he always painted me sad, disturbed, and distressed as a symbol of the war in Spain, but that was not his real intent. He portrayed me that way to tell the world that I was a weak and lesser being. But those portraits were false.

I am an artist in full, a creator of images that, once seen, can never be forgotten. My portrait of Père Ubu. "The Pretender." "Shampooing." All those images and more I made long before Pablo came into my life. He had seen my photos of the streets of Paris, the rag picker, the mannequin in the window, the man with his head under the sidewalk, long before we met in Les Deux Magots. He witnessed my power that day as I sat at a table jabbing a penknife between my splayed fingers. Fast, faster, faster still, only missing slightly once or twice to bring a drop of blood to adorn the roses embroidered on my black gloves. Pablo begged me for those gloves. He locked them in a case where he kept his other love trophies.

I was his official mistress, but I challenged as much as inspired him. I was not his muse, I was his teacher, although he would never admit it. I urged him to paint "Guernica" after the bombing. I pushed him to do it and documented his work in photographs while he created it. I even made many of the brush marks that formed the dying horse in the center of the work.

I had studied painting, of course, and moved easily back and forth from the canvas to the darkroom. Pablo encouraged me to pour my energies into a paint brush instead of my camera, a suggestion motivated, I'm sure, by his supreme confidence that I could never beat him at his own game. That question was unanswered when he left me floating in the void.

His departure should have been a relief to me, a release of unbearable tension. The flagrant jealousy over my work. The endless arguments about Olga, his wife. The actual, real, physical fights with Marie Therese, the mother of his illegitimate daughter. He egged the two of us on to combat, then stood by laughing while we pulled and shoved and slapped each other mindlessly.

When he left, all that cruelty should have ended, but it didn't. I warred with his other lovers in my imagination and I fought him in absentia. I battled myself until I entered the asylum. The violence ended only when the doctors strapped me to their cold hard table and pummeled my brain into convulsive seizures that drove Pablo Picasso from my mind. After Picasso, there was only God.

I became a person I no longer recognized and I retreated to my house in Menerbes with its green shutters and views of Mont Ventoux. I gazed on the Luberon valley, painted the landscapes with shallow smears and soft caresses, and let the colors become what they wished. I hand-tinted negatives to make purely abstract prints in the darkroom. Creating images without a camera was for me the ultimate marriage of art and life. I stayed out of the public eye, showed no one my work, and devoted the last half of my life to realizing my vision.

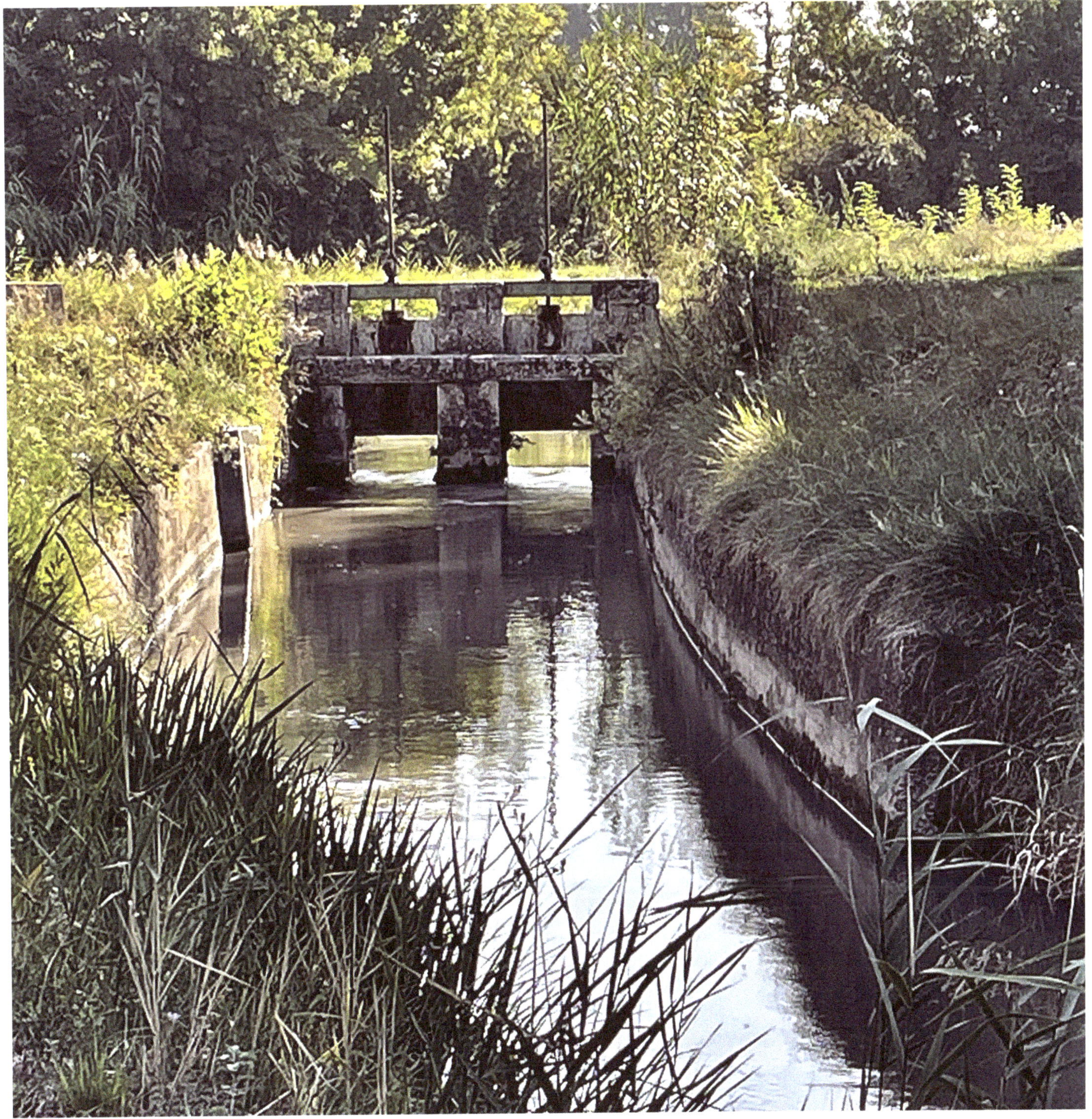

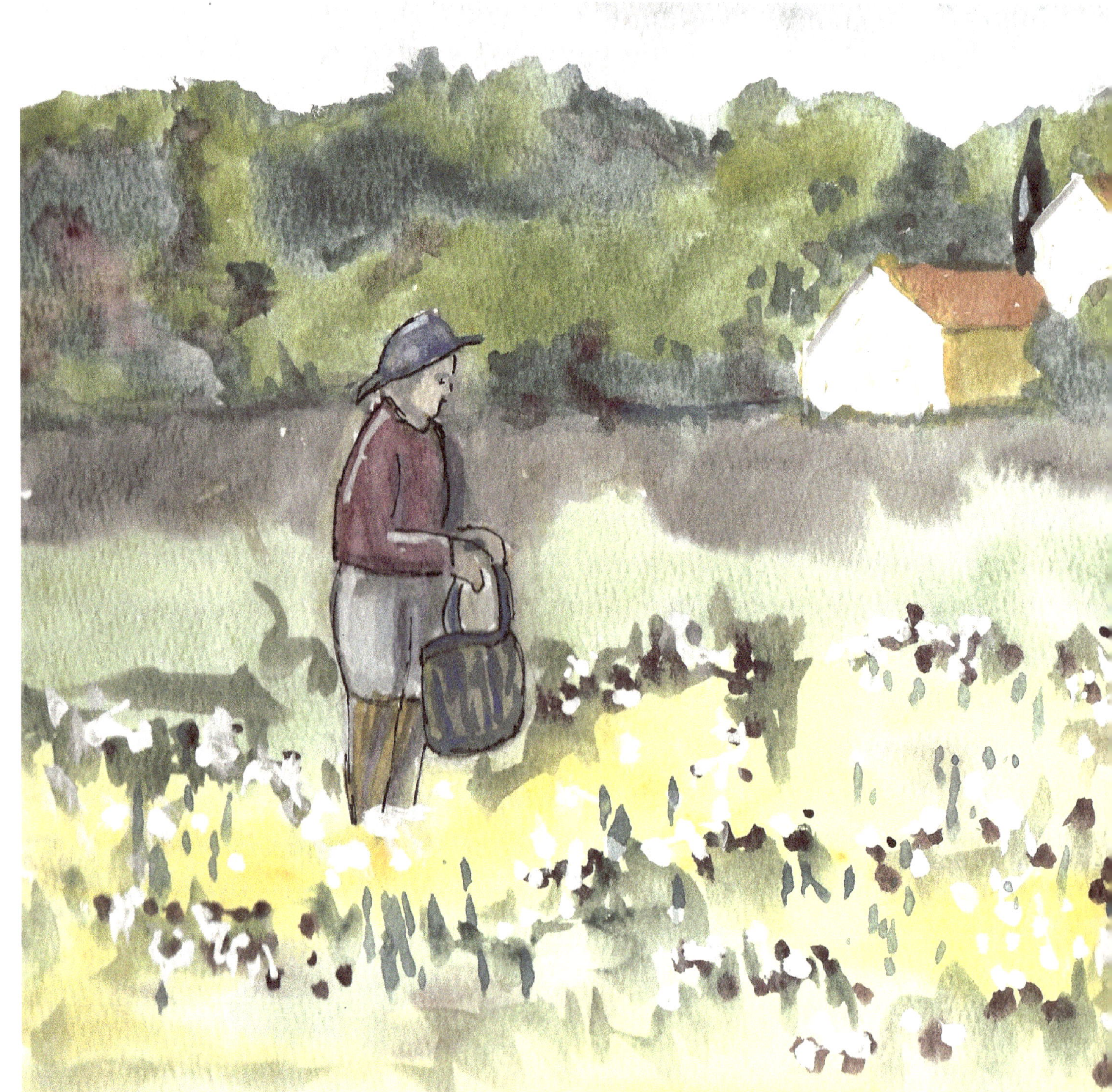

Field of Life

It is simple, this life
Tomatoes and basil
Olive oil and garlic
A baguette
Perhaps a chop
Caressed by butter
And parsley
Season after season
The earth feeds
The rain baptizes
The sun blesses
Might there be wine?

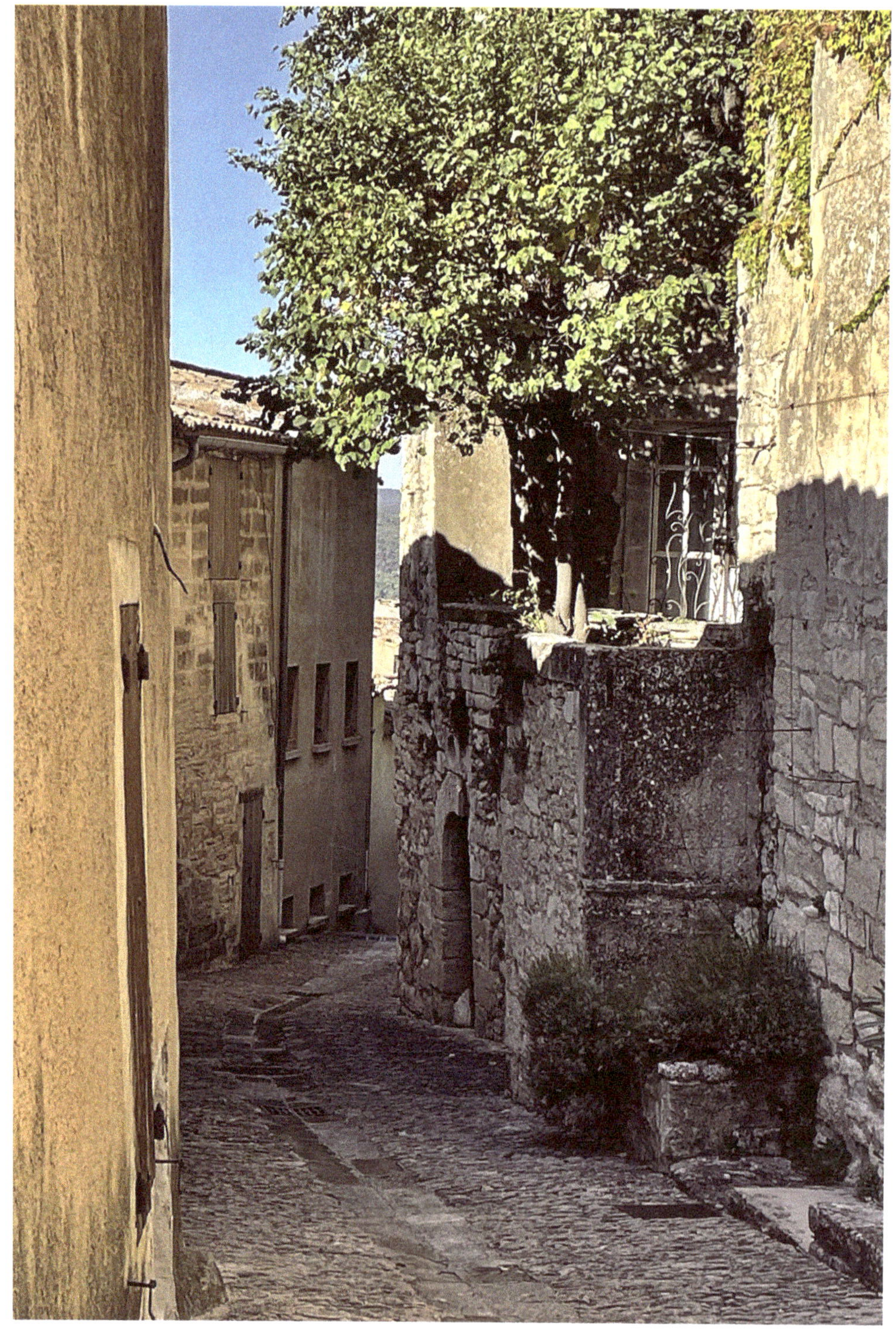

Chapter Six

Red Furrows

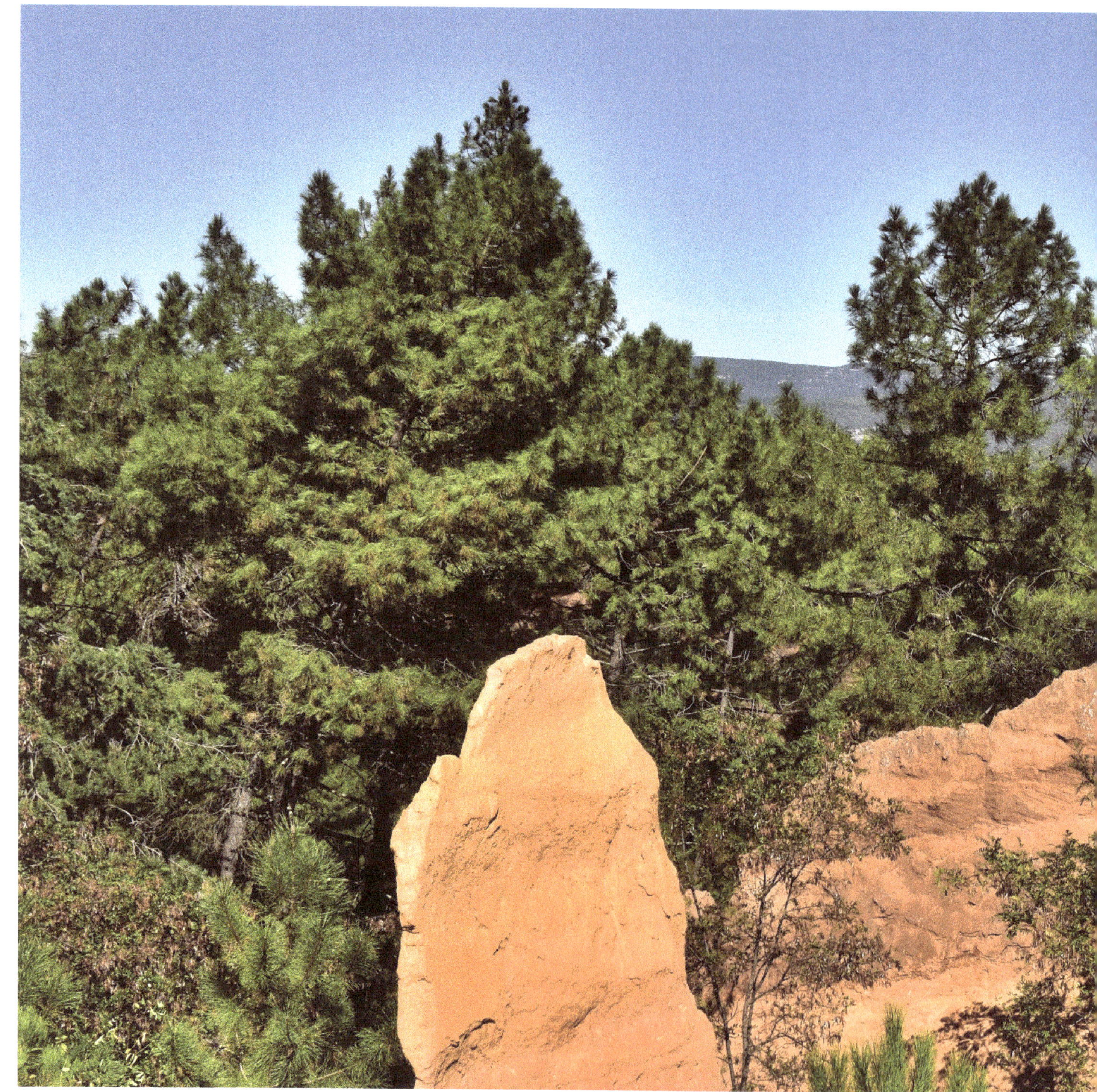

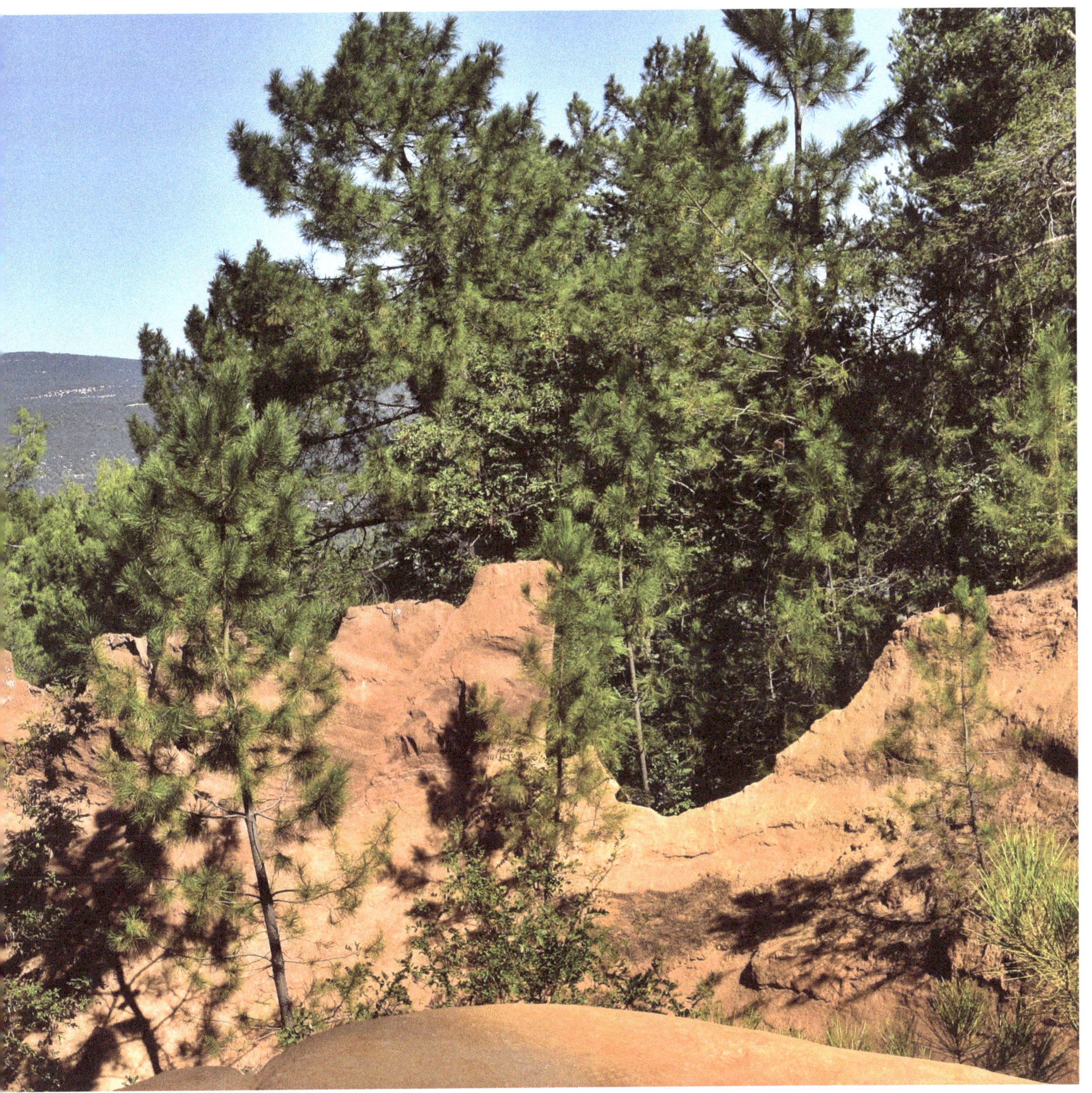

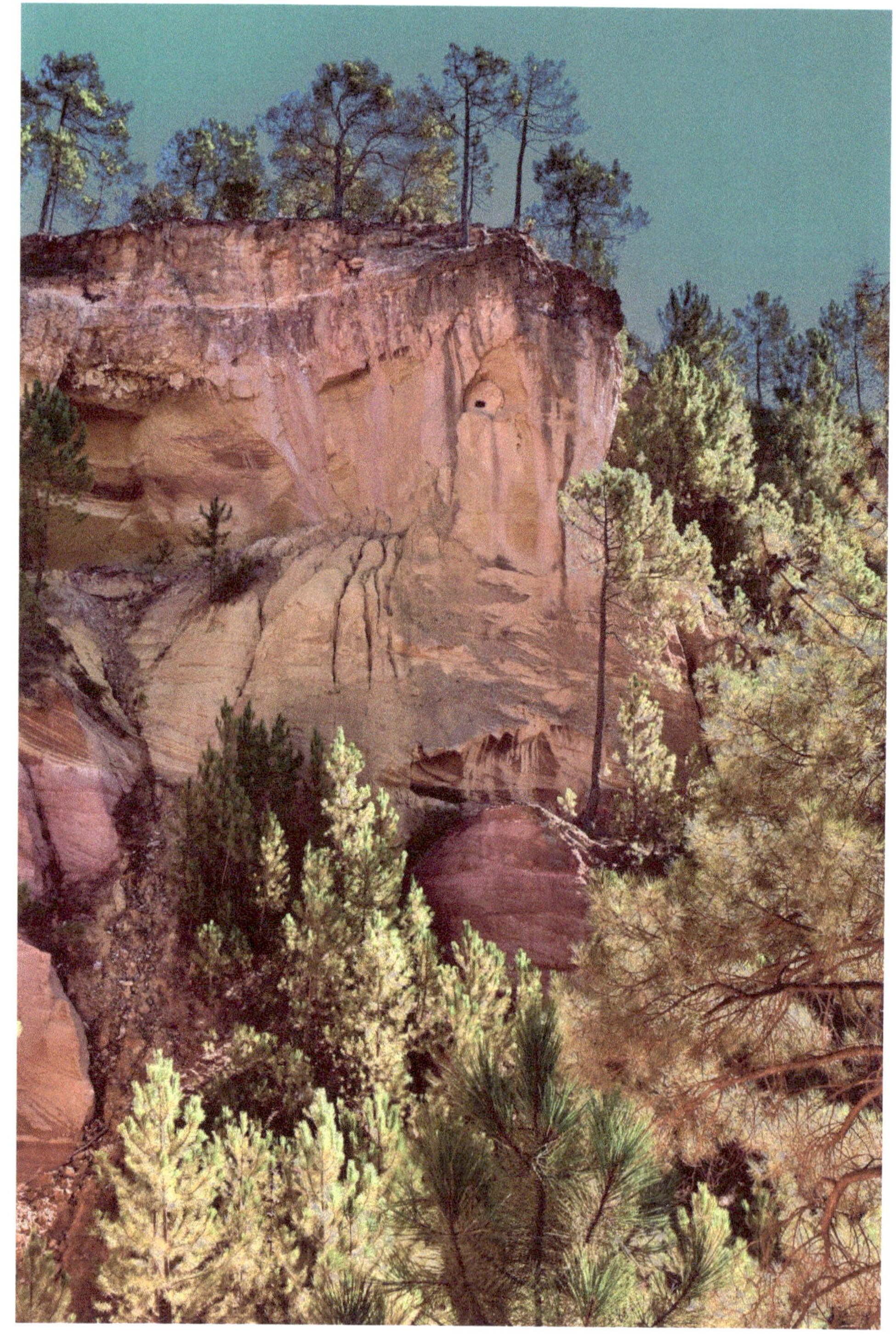

Roussillon

According to legend, the colorful shades of ochre permeating Roussillon aren't natural. It all supposedly began when Guillame de Cabestan came to Roussillon to apprentice in the castle of Lady Sermonde and her husband, Lord Raymond d'Avignon. Lord Raymond, it seems, preferred the company of horses and his huntsmen, and often left his wife alone at home while he roamed far and wide across the countryside. The young Guillame soon filled the vacancy her husband left in the lady's heart. He began composing songs about their love that aroused the suspicions of the servants, who took their tales to Lord Raymond.

When Lord Raymond accused Guillame, the lad deftly told him that the servants were mistaken—his songs of love were dedicated to Lady Sermonde's sister, Agnes. To learn the truth, Lord Raymond went to query the sister with Guillame in tow. When Guillame pledged his love to her, Agnes saw through his ruse but played along with it for the sake of her sister. Lord Raymond was appeased and all seemed well.

Lady Sermonde, however, was furious with Guillame for denying their love. She demanded that he compose a song declaring she was his one true love. When the besotted young man did as he was told, unfortunately, Lord Raymond overheard the tune and invited Guillame to accompany him on a hunt. Once in the woods, Lord Raymond stabbed the lad and chopped off his head. He then cut out his heart and took it back to the castle where he ordered his cook to prepare it in a spicy stew to be served to Lady Sermonde.

When the dame told the cook she found the stew quite tasty, her husband laid Guillame's head on the table before her and revealed that she had just eaten her lover's heart.

"Seigneur," she reportedly said, "You have given me such a fine meal that I wish to never eat anything else again." With those final words, Lady Sermonde flew out of the castle to the edge of the cliff where she threw herself to immortality. A spring gushed forth from the spot where she landed and her blood, it is said, dyed the land around for miles and miles.

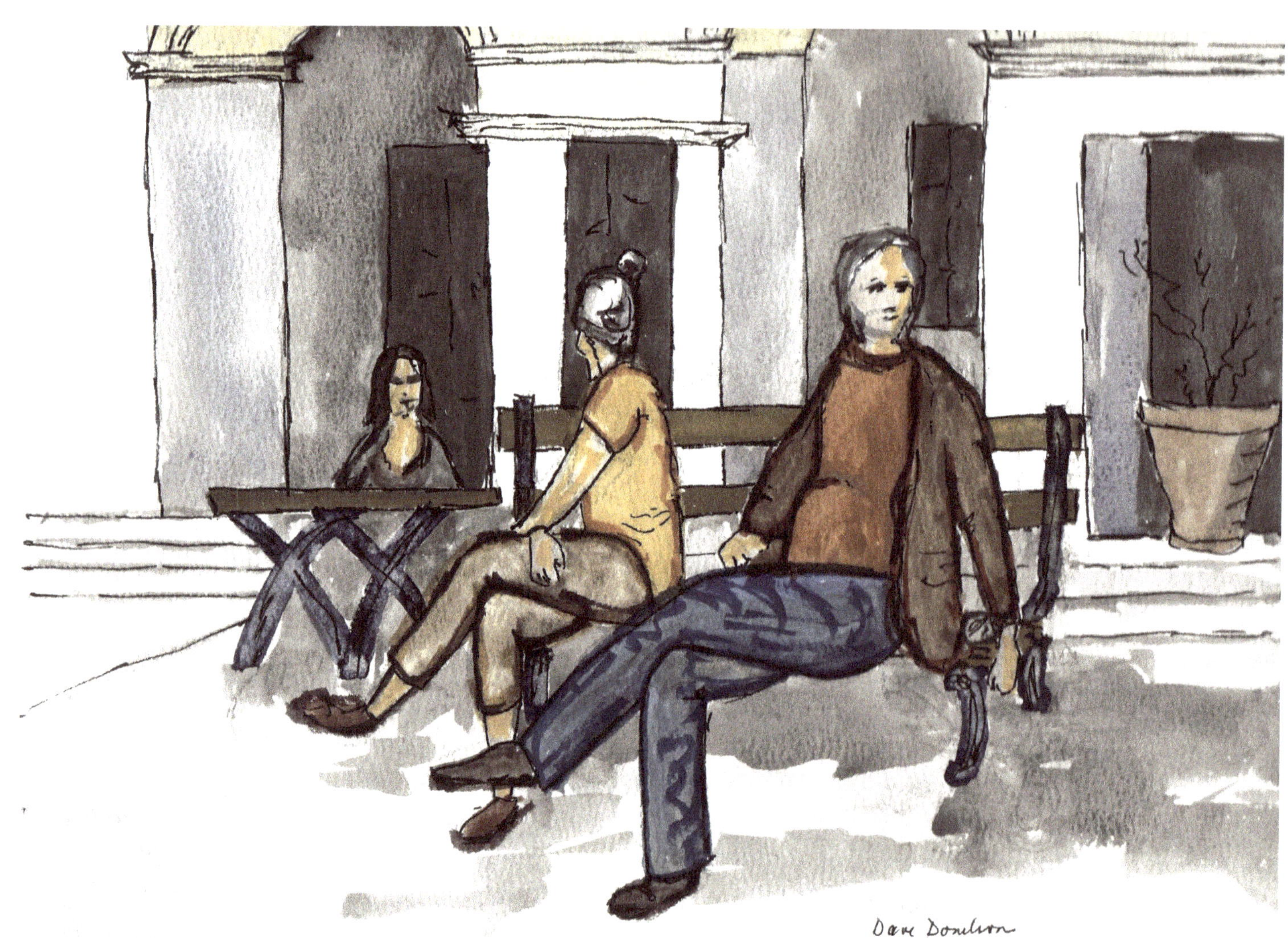

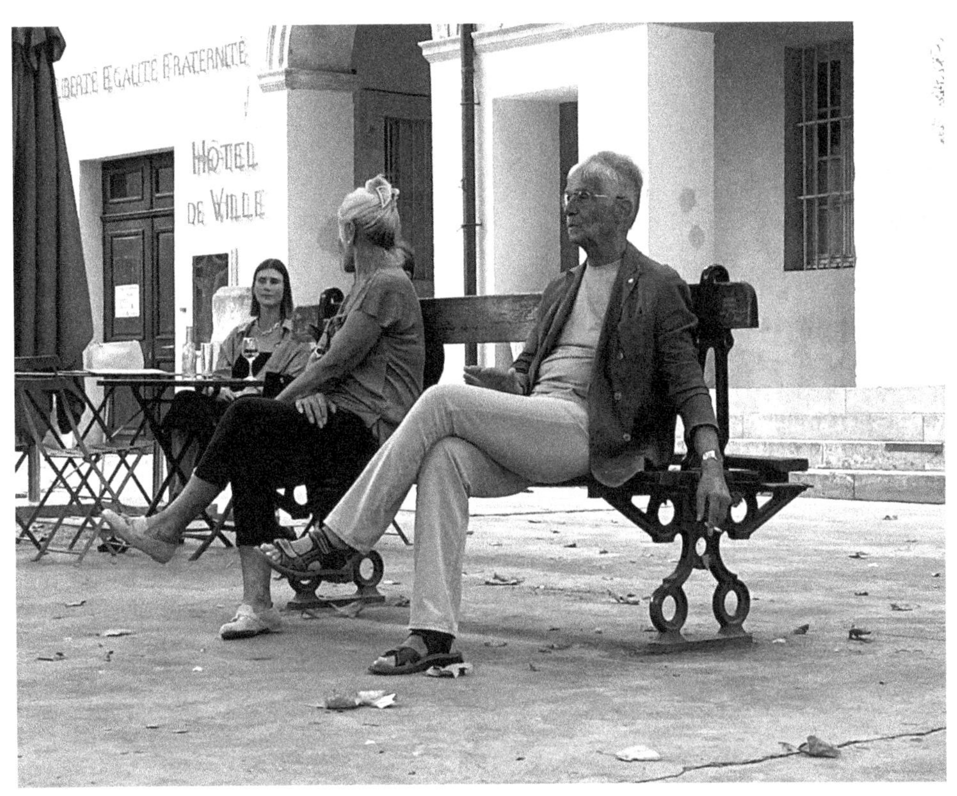
IBERTÉ ÉGALITÉ FRATERNITÉ
HÔTEL
DE VILLE

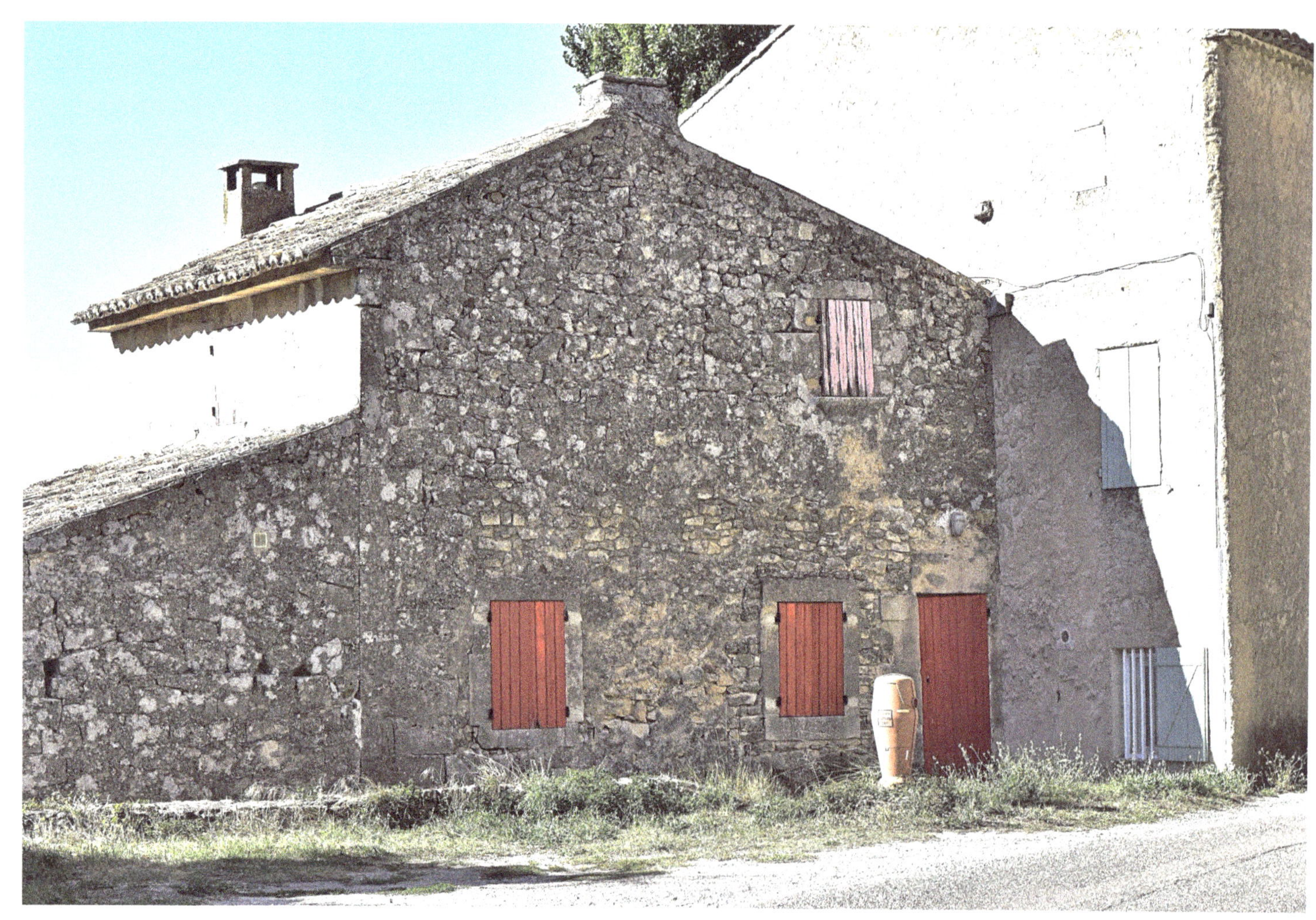

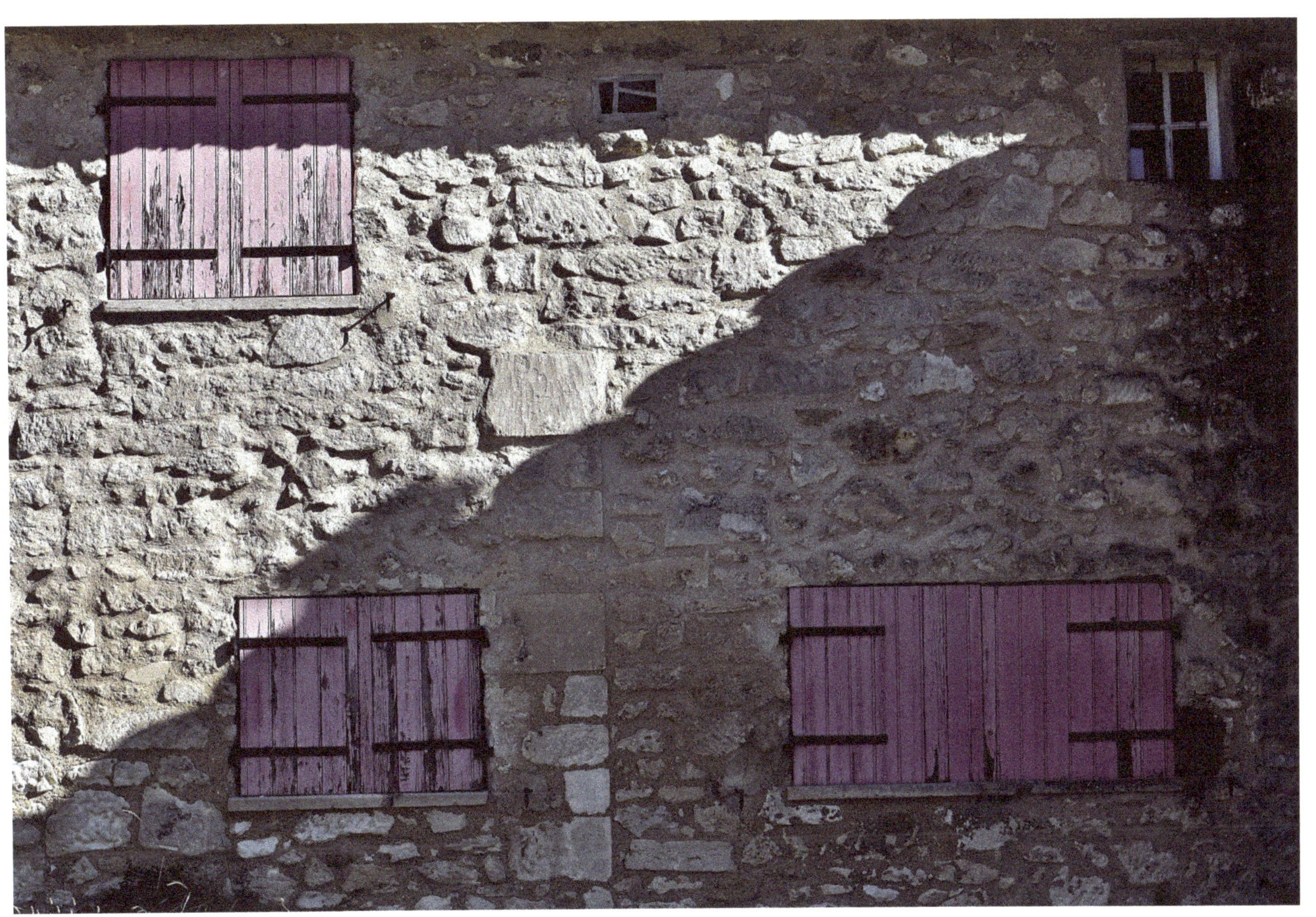

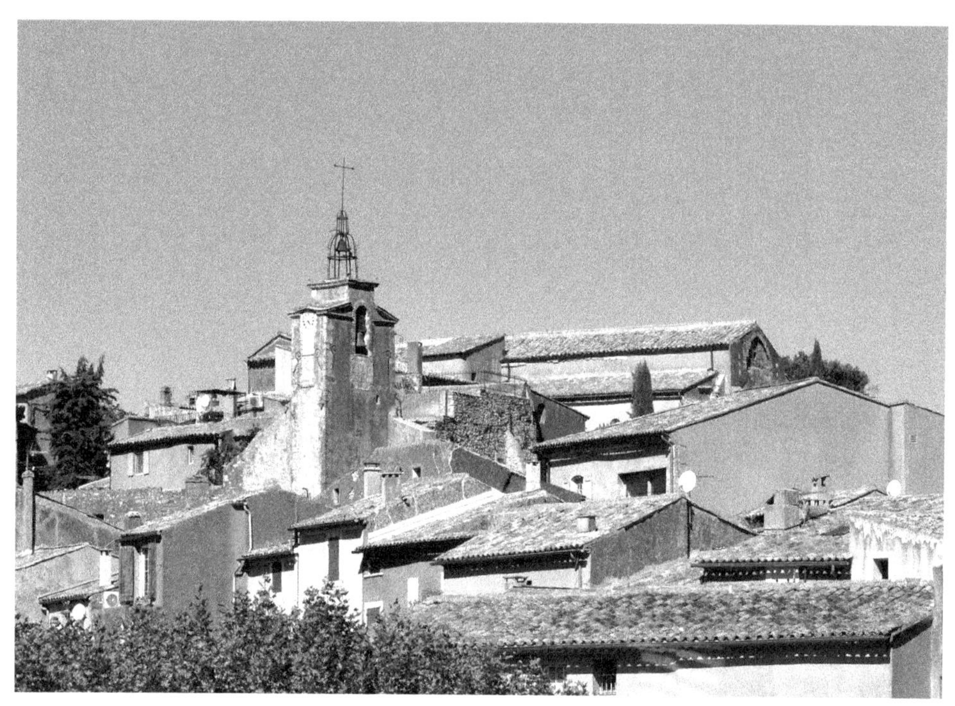

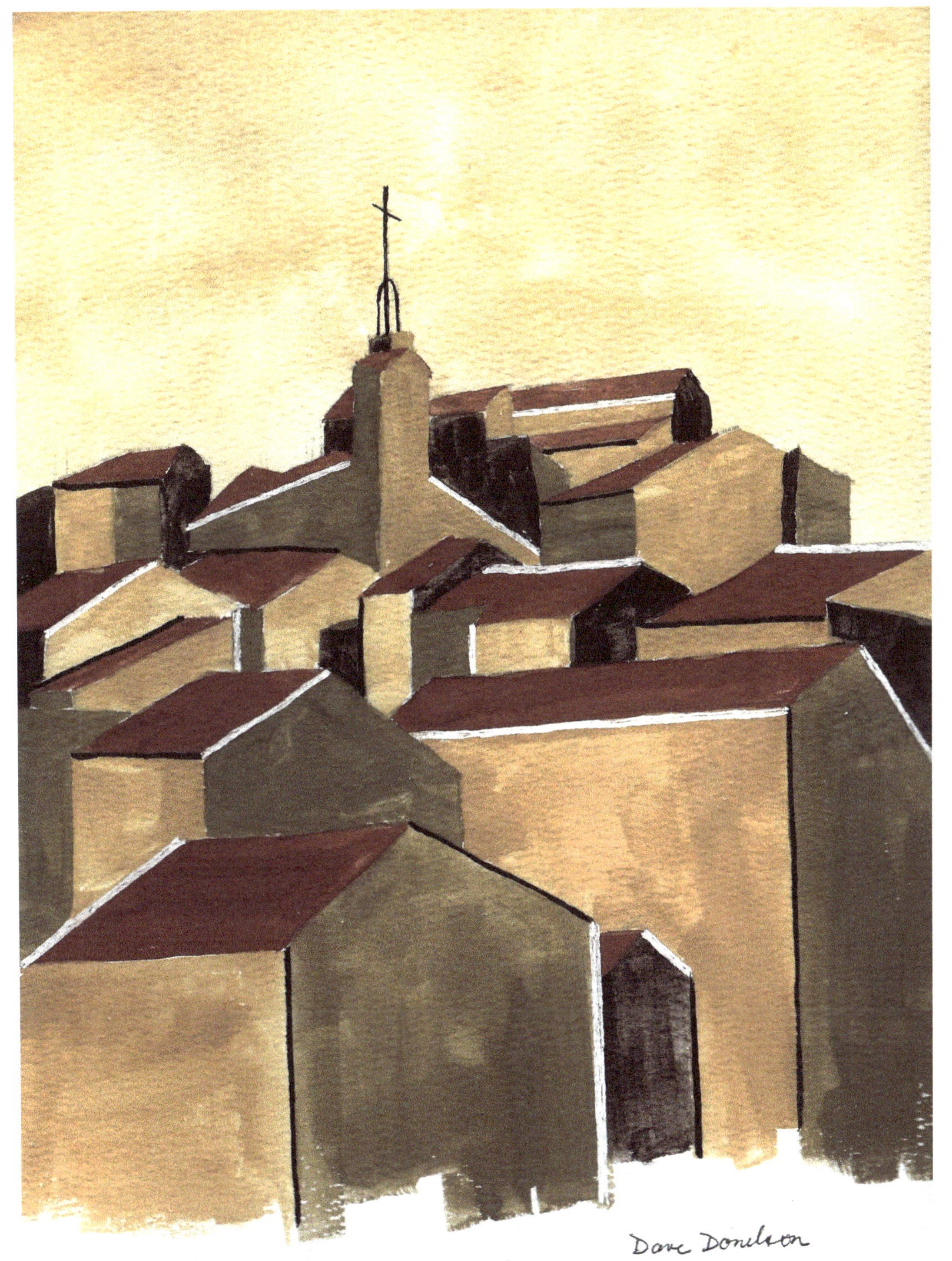
Dave Donelson

Ode to Ochre

We wander the rust canyons of Roussillon
Where the earth coughs ochre
A sun of rust dyeing the dirt
Red, yellow, umber, orange
Sunshine driven into the earth
To ferment and form the solids
That coat the miners' sweaty bodies
When they scrape it into their baskets
And carry it to stain the mortar stone
With its red breath
To braise the pestle with
Its golden perspiration
To fog the fingers with
Its russet respiration
The ochre stalks the pallet
Hunting for a way home
Canvas becomes its earth

I find ochre pigments in
Tiny boxes holding shades
of the washed yellow of midday
the burnt black of midnight
Golds, reds, and browns prevail
Yellow and black yield green
gray and red bring violet
but there is no natural blue
The values are deep
A spot of pigment goes a very long way
I mix a drop of gum arabic in honey
then add water for consistency
and fall in love with it on the paper

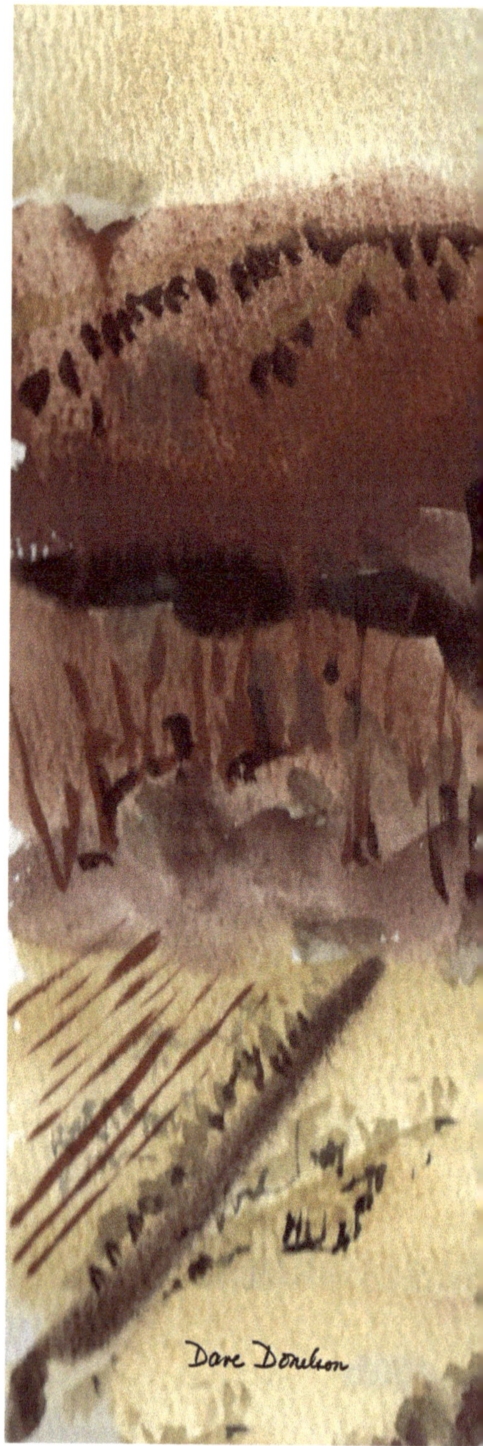

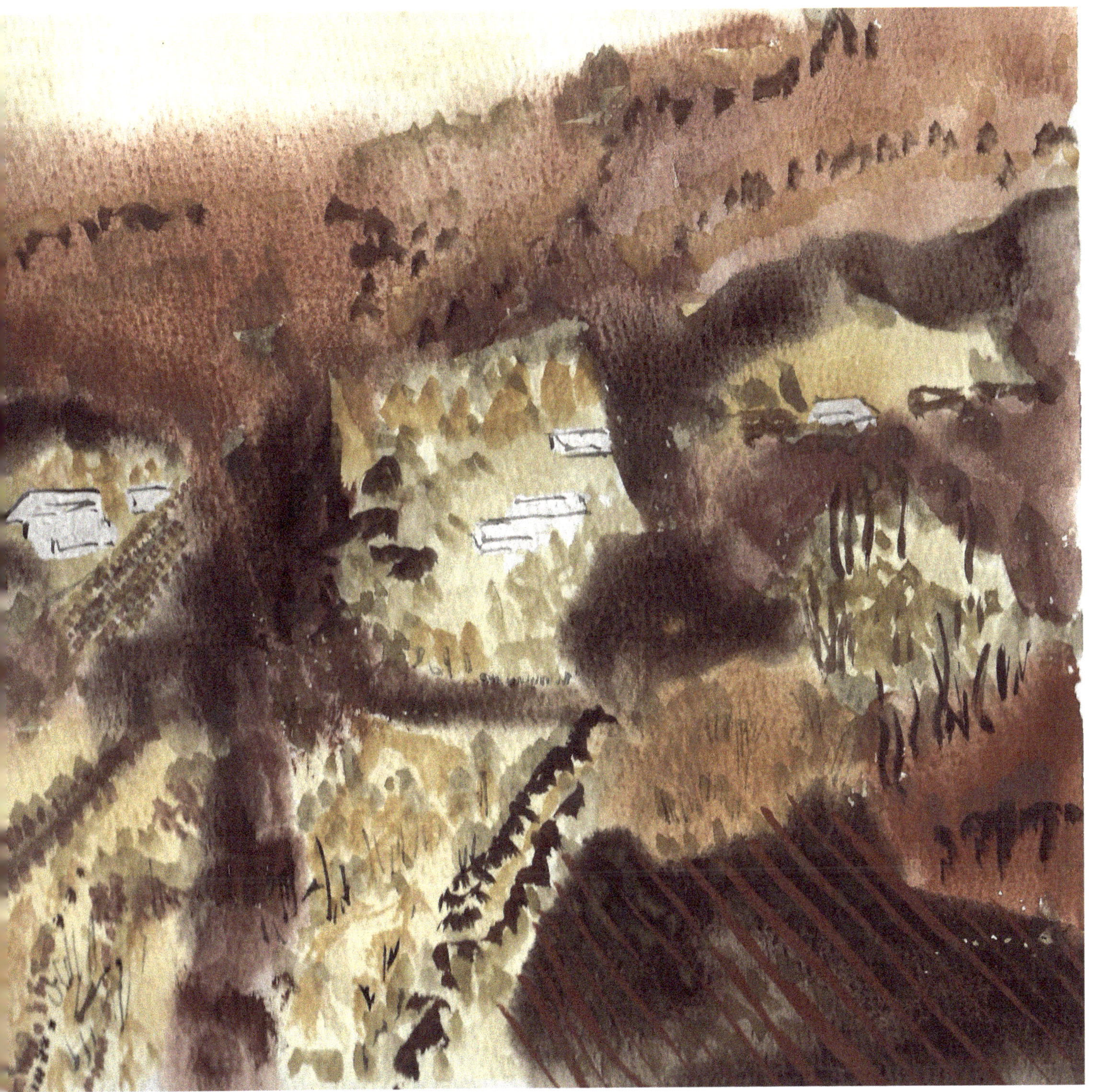

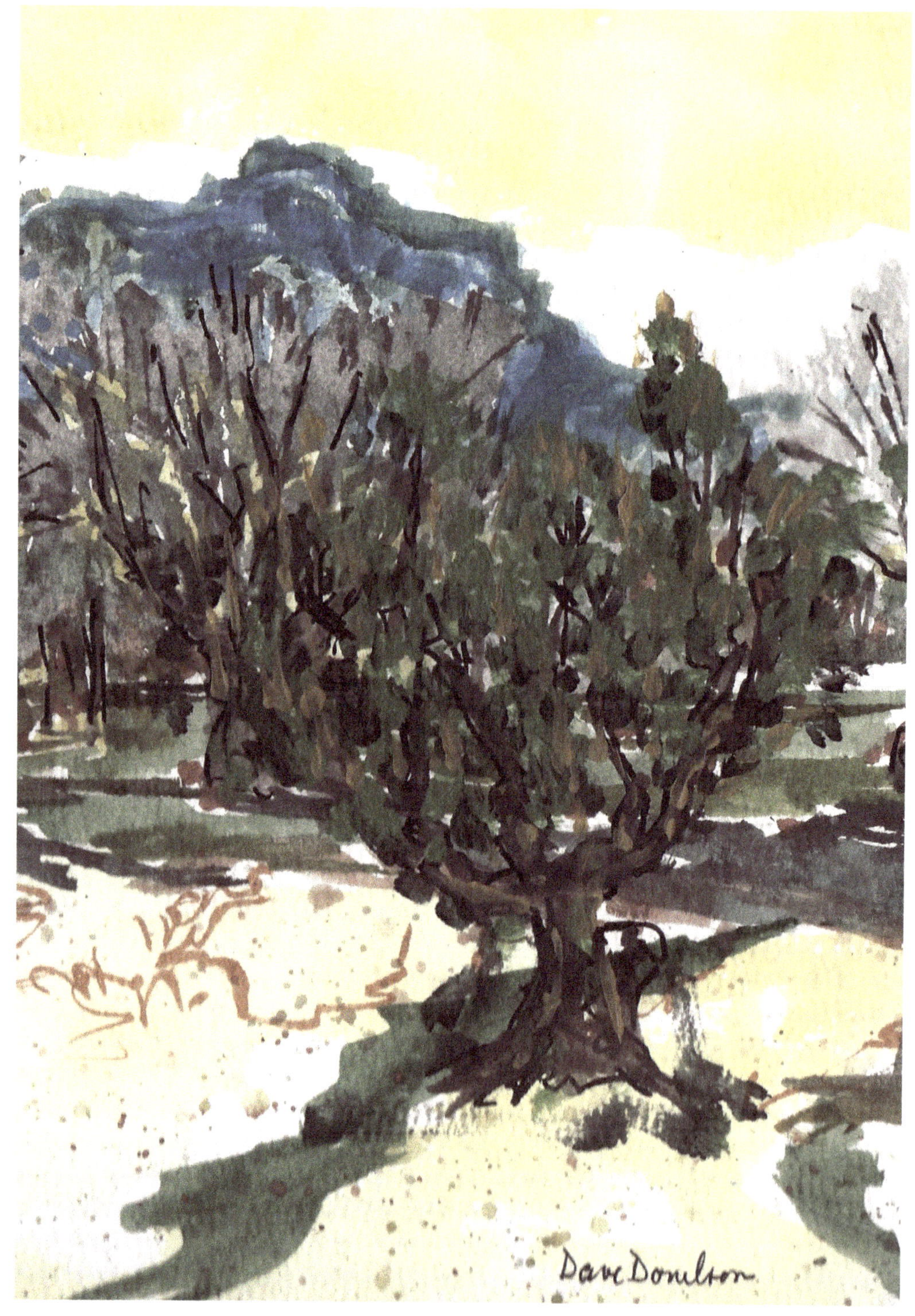
Dave Donelson

Chapter Seven
Solace

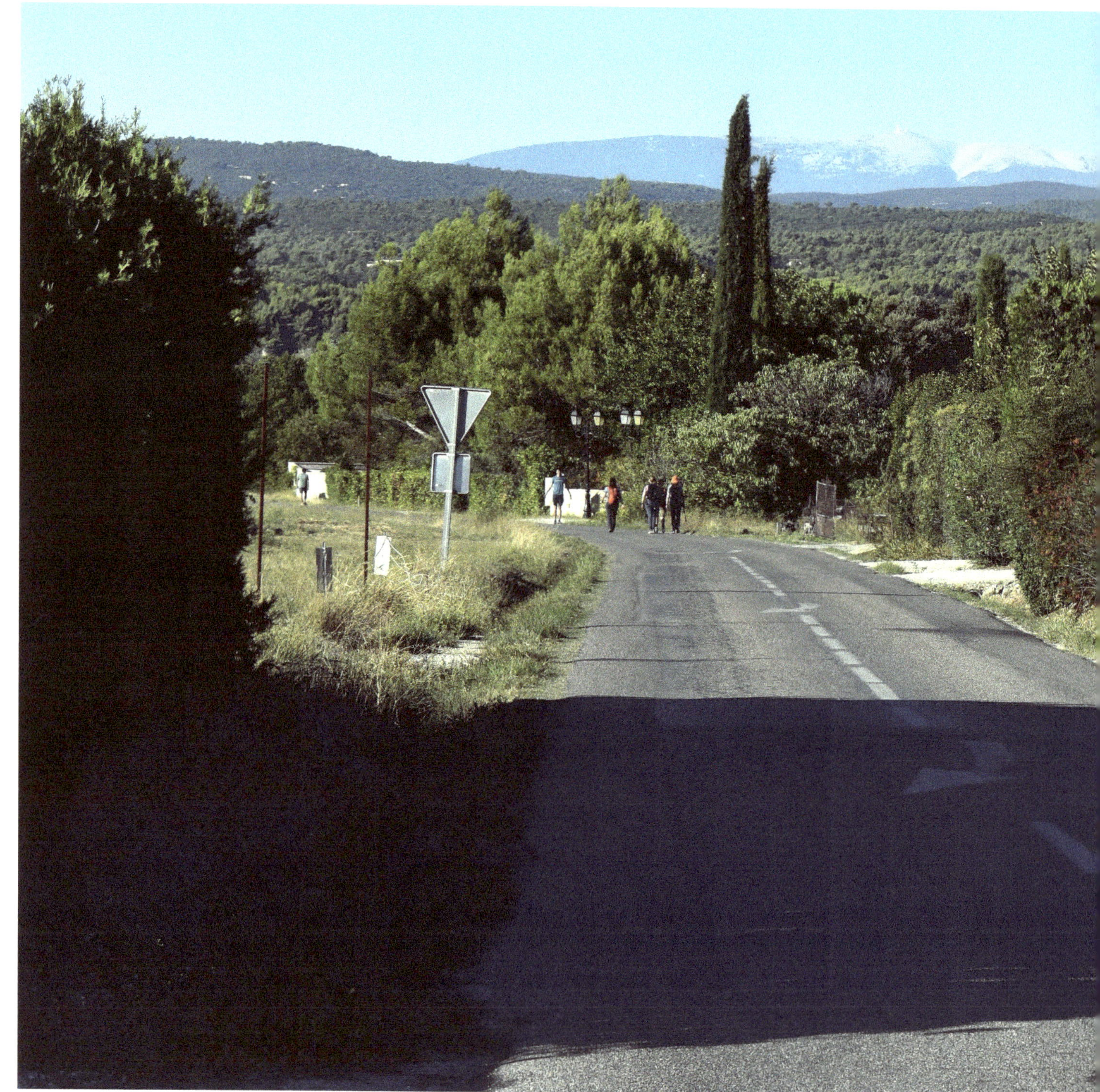

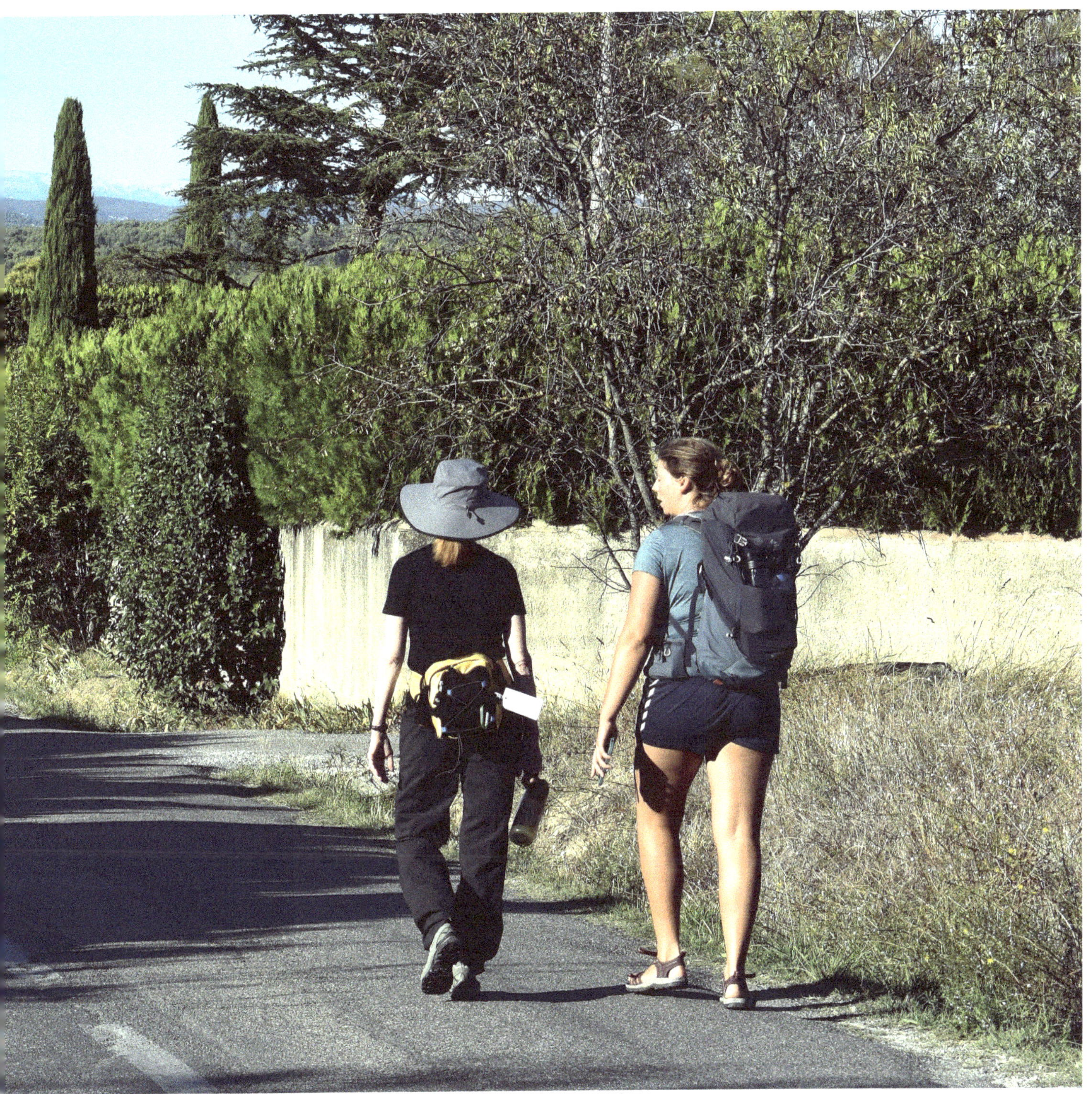

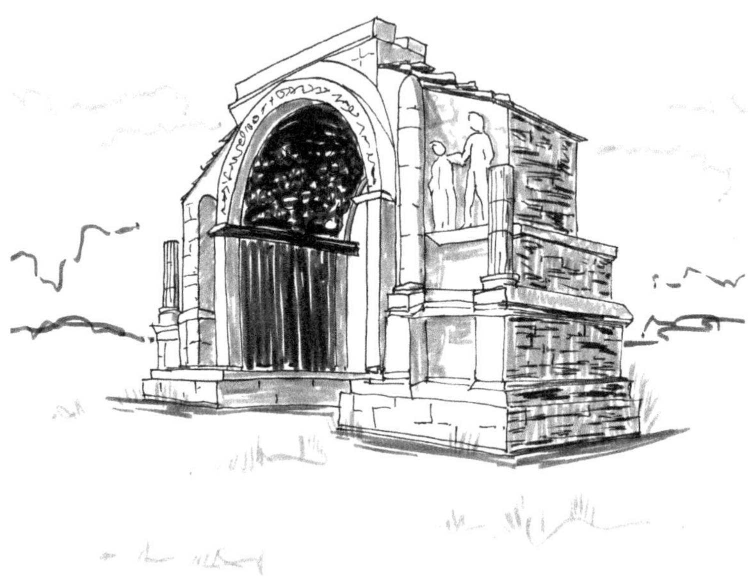

Glanum

The ruins of the Roman city of Glanum lie on the southern outskirts of St. Remy, just a short walk from the asylum where Vincent Van Gogh voluntarily spent a year of his life. Before the Romans came, it was a Celto-Ligurian village built around a spring reputed to have healing powers. The village was destroyed by the Romans in 125 BC, but the region wasn't secured until Julius Caesar captured Marseille in 49 BC.

Glanum prospered and grew under Roman rule and a triumphal arch was constructed just outside its northern gate in 10 BC. The arch commemorated Roman civilization and served as a warning to Rome's enemies. The arch still stands, as does the Mausoleum of the Julii, erected to honor a local family that received Roman citizenship in return for their service to the state.

Glanum was overrun and destroyed by the Alamanni in 260 AD. The inhabitants abandoned the site and moved north into the plain where they founded the city that is today St. Remy.

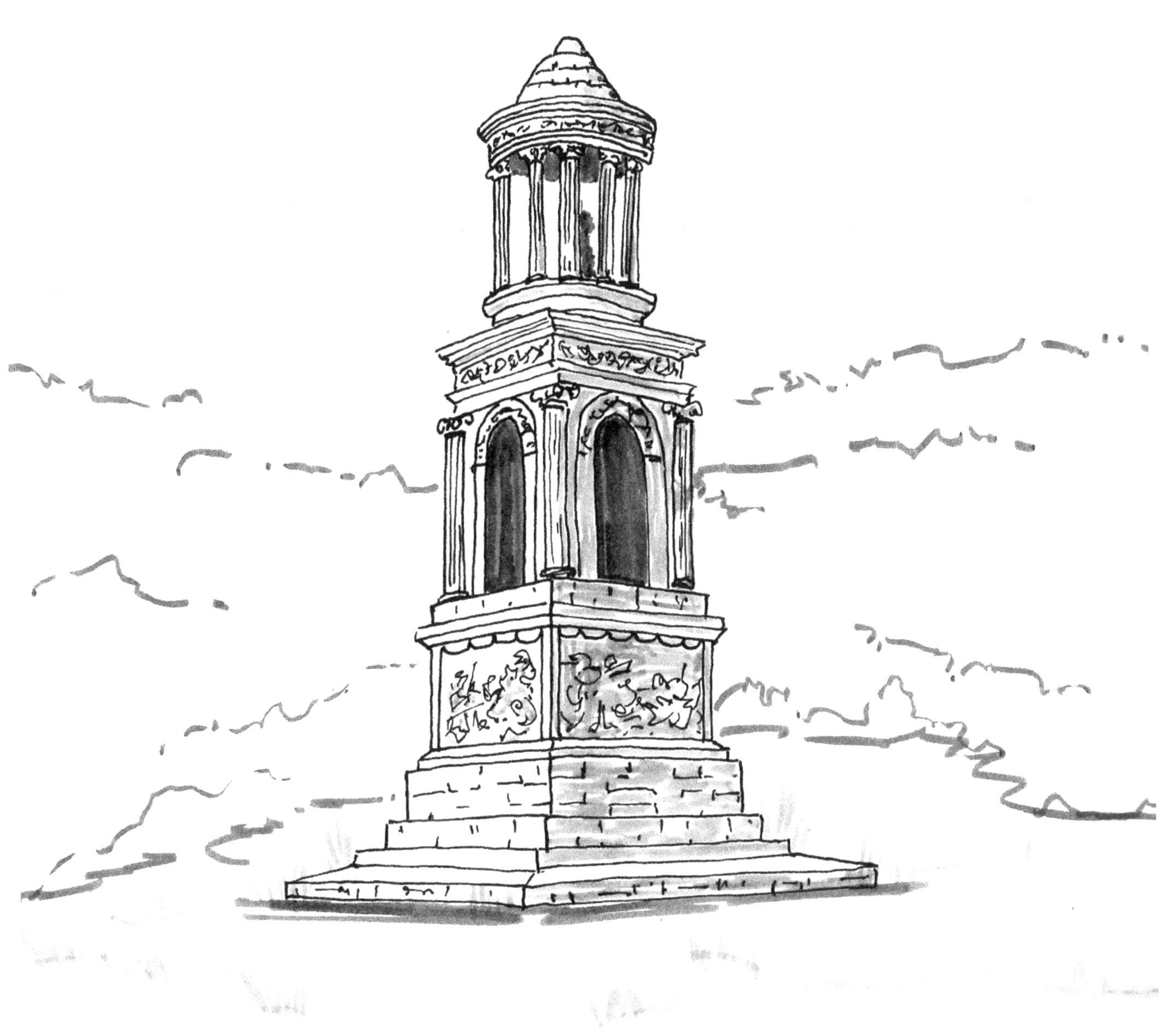

Asylum

Vincent Van Gogh lived for just one year in the Asylum of St. Paul near St. Remy, but what a year it was. During those twelve months, despite being confined to his rooms when he first arrived and too ill to paint for several long spells later, he completed some 150 paintings and hundreds of drawings and sketches. A month after he was admitted, he painted what many consider his magnum opus, "Starry Night." The painting was done from memory in his room, and features the sky as seen from his east-facing window over an imaginary village.

Painting was his solace, especially scenes from nature, the budding flowers that promised rebirth, the wheat fields and olive groves that marked the changing of the seasons, the stalwart trees on the asylum grounds that symbolized protection. He wrote to his mother, "But for one's health, as you say, it is very necessary to work in the garden and see the flowers growing."

While confined to his rooms, he portrayed their interiors as well as what he could see from his windows, the asylum gardens and the wheat fields and olive groves beyond. When allowed to go outside, he studied the buildings and trees, often adding enigmatic figures to the scenes. From nearly everywhere, he could see Mont Gaussier, which can be found in many landscapes.

Near the end of his stay, he devoted hours to creating some of his best-known still lifes including "Irises" and "Vase with Irises Against a Yellow Background." He wrote to his sister, Wil, "The last days in St. Remy I worked like a madman. Great bouquets of flowers, violet-colored irises, great bouquets of roses."

The work Van Gogh completed during his stay in the asylum finally earned him a touch of recognition he had long been denied. His devoted brother, Theo, placed several of those works in major exhibitions in Brussels. A scene painted near Arles just before he fled the town, "The Red Vineyard," was purchased by artist Anna Boch at the seventh exhibition of *Les XX* in January, 1890, a few months before Van Gogh left the asylum at St. Remy. It was the only sale of a painting made during his lifetime.

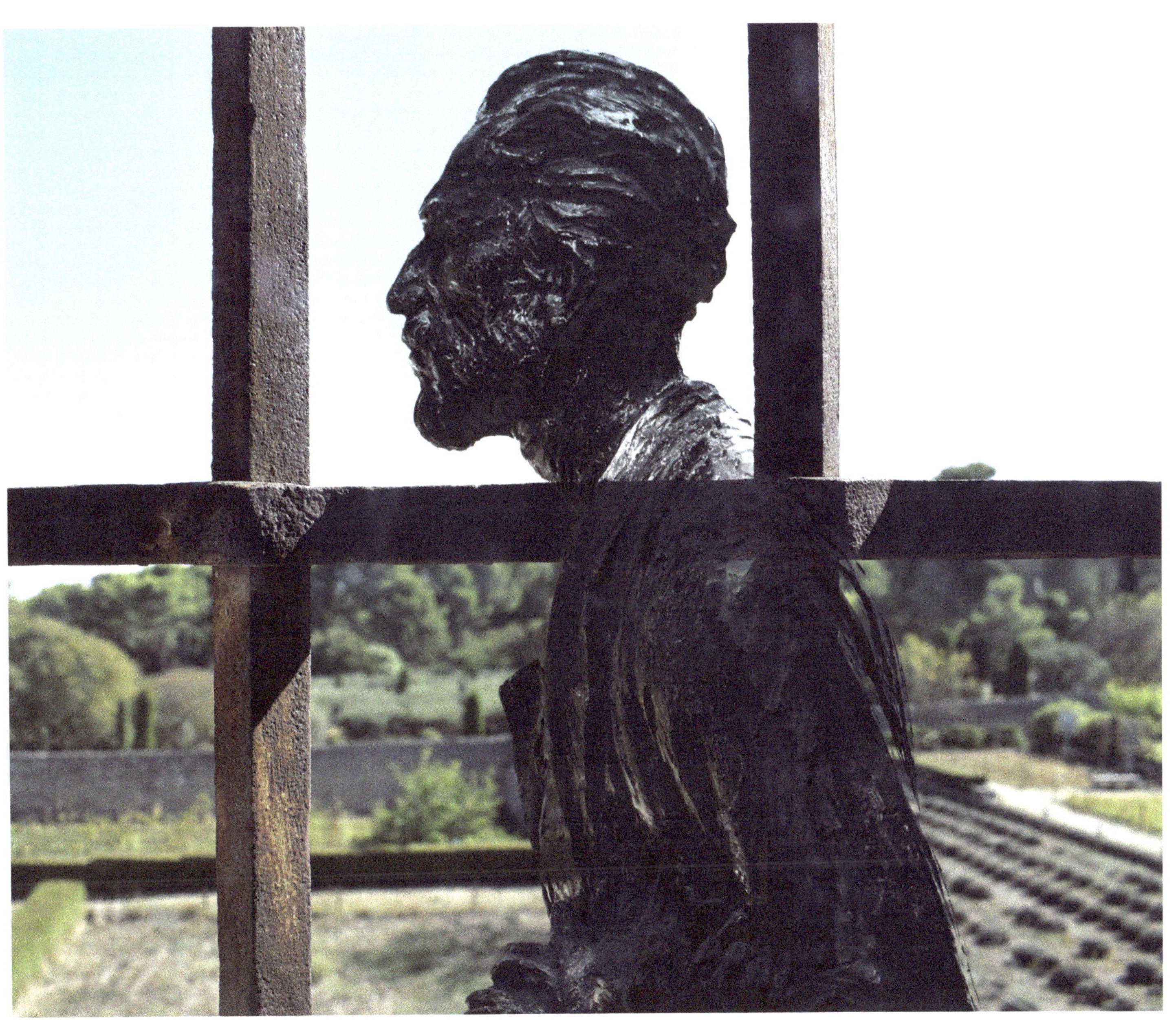

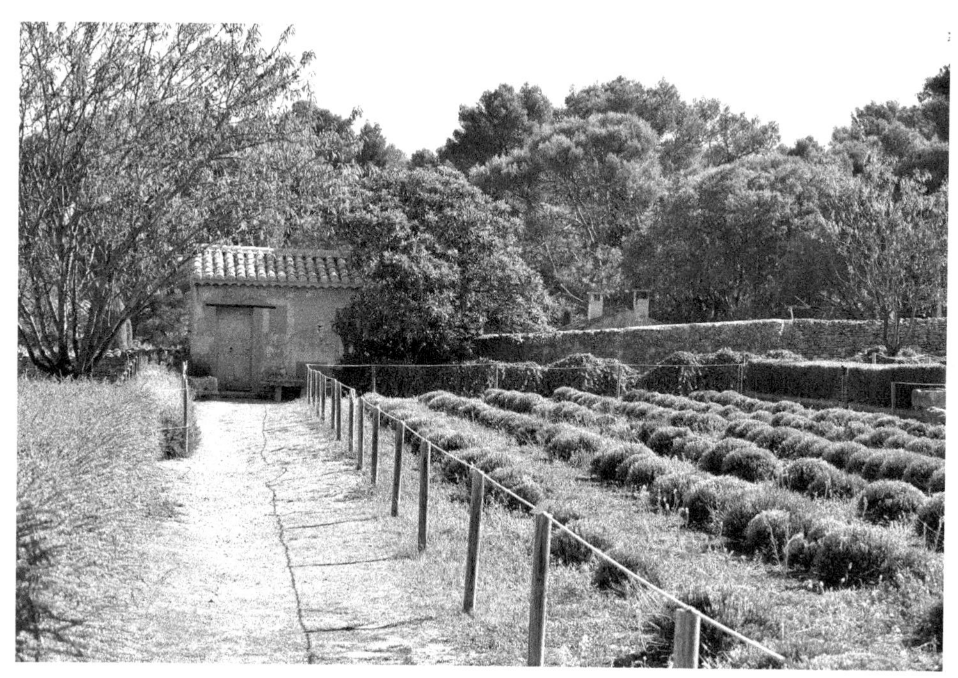

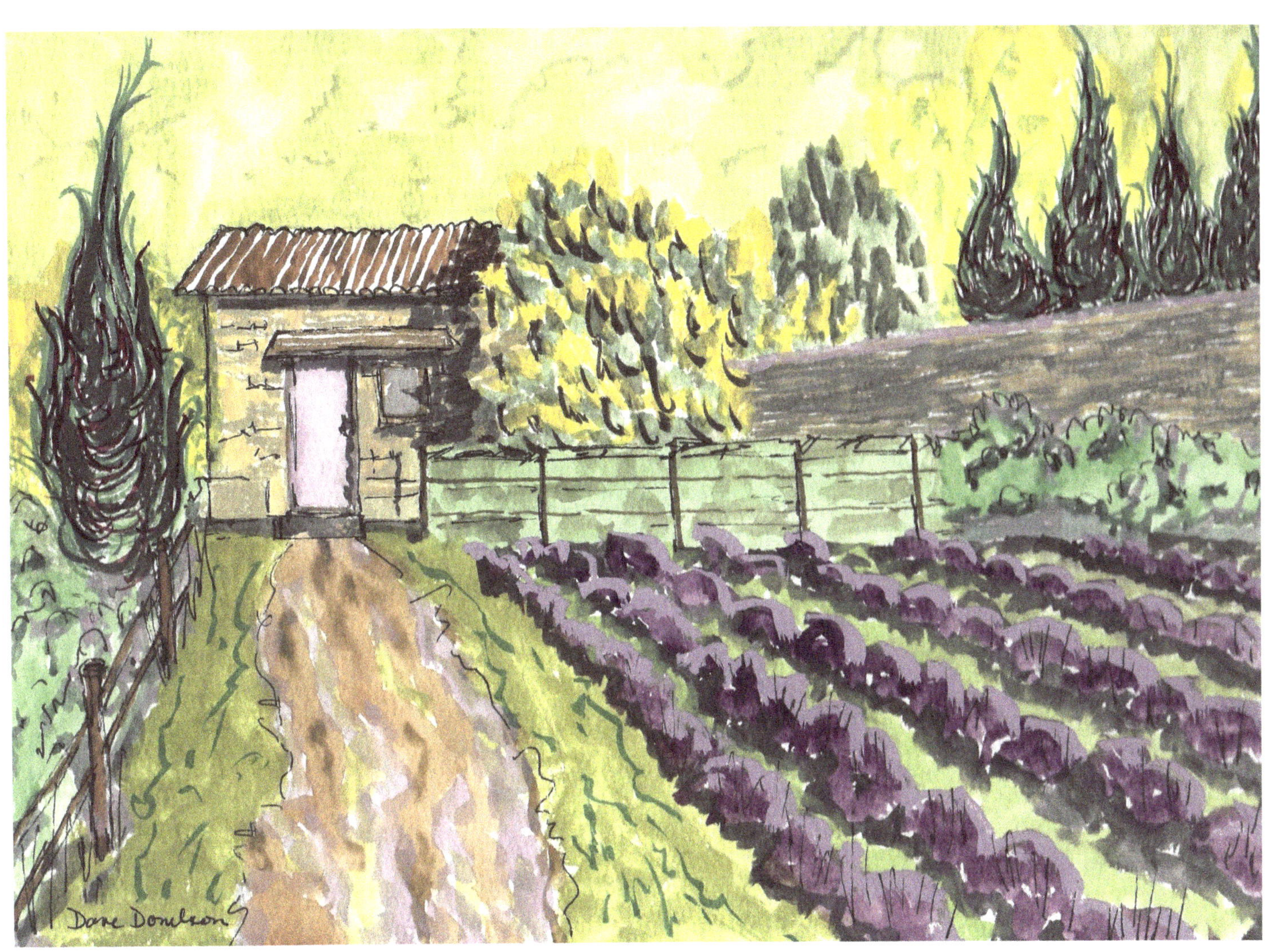

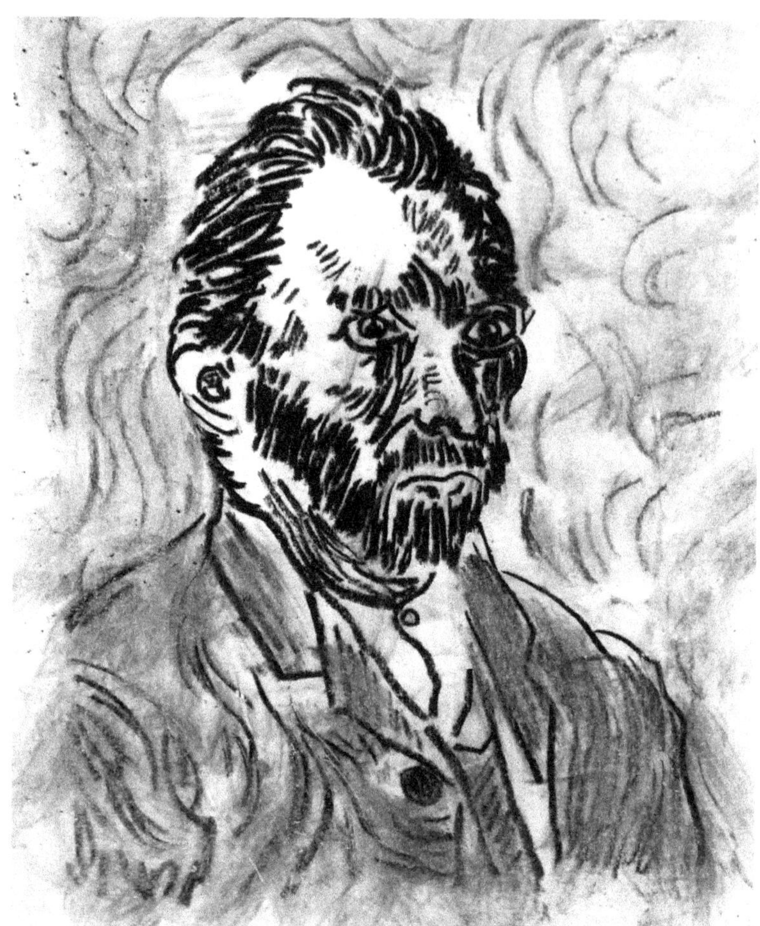

Interview with Vincent In the Asylum

Q: Why did you come to Provence, Vincent?

A: To grow as an artist and become a better person. My life has been one sad failure after another. I disappointed everyone. I thought the change would help.

Q: And what happened when you arrived?

A: I began working like one actually possessed. More than ever, I was in a dumb fury of work. And I thought it would help cure me.

Q: Cure you of what?

A: It is hard to describe, but I know it was rooted in my own work. I was risking my life for it and my reason had half-foundered because of it.

Q. And moving to Provence helped? How so?

A: I found wonderous light with a vague consonance of colors which are at last right in feeling. The sun here drowns everything in a pure golden light. I devour it. It fills my ears and I hear it sing. It eats my bones, but in a good way. The light is all, you know. It is the all of all painting, of all seeing, the all of my everything.

Q: Did it help you?

A: Oh yes, the light here helped me see, to move with its rhythms. Light has tempo, you know. It swirls and twirls all around and leaves trails in the ether. When I release myself to it, the light guides my brush and paint across the canvas.

Q: That's fascinating. Did it make you a better person, too?

A: It did at first, but then Paul came and we argued. In the beginning, I thought he came to live alongside me, to tighten the bonds of our friendship. But I suspect now he came only to please Theo so that Theo would buy more of his paintings. You know Gaugin. He was only here for nine weeks, but he wanted to take charge of everything. The studio, our work day by day, even me. I tried and tried to get along with him, but he said he couldn't live with my obsessions. But art is my obsession! My life! I would lose myself if I gave in to him.

Q: What happened?

A: He left. I tried to stop him. I was shaving when he went out the door, and I followed him with my razor in my hand. I promised to change, but he didn't believe me. I wept and pleaded with him to stay, but he pushed me away. He had a knife, a sword maybe. I don't know. I was frantic.

Q: And then?

A: He ran away and I discovered my ear had been slashed. Red blood flowed down my neck. My ear lobe came off as I staunched the blood with a white napkin. I went to get help and came across a girl I know, Gabrielle, who cleaned a brothel in the neighborhood. I don't know what happened to the white napkin with my ear. Maybe I gave it to her. Maybe she knocked it from my hand. When I try to remember, all is black.

Q: Your life took a major turn at that time, didn't it?

A: Yes, everyone thought I was mad. Maybe I was. Maybe I still am. I don't know. The townspeople feared me even before that happened. They mocked me as I roamed the countryside with my easel and brushes and canvases searching for subjects to paint. When Gaugin left, they signed a petition to remove me from my home in the yellow house. It all became too much, so I came here to the asylum.

Q: Do you feel better now?

A: Oh yes, I could stay here quite a long time. Never have I been as tranquil as here, able at last to paint a little.

Q: You do not feel mad? Are you cured?

A: I hope I have had no more than the simple passing crisis of an artist.

Q: And how do you find the light in St. Remy?

A: It is even better. Or maybe I am simply seeing it more vividly. That happens, sometimes, you know. I get excited and, well, overly excited at times. But the light here has never failed me. Except when…

Q: Except?

A: Except when I cannot leave my room. When they won't let me. Or sometimes when I need to hide.

Q: Hide? From whom?

A: From myself or others. I'd rather not talk about it. It'd rather talk about the light and the colors and my painting.

Q: Of course. You even paint in your room, do you not? What do you paint?

A: Ha! I paint whatever I can see. I look through the bars and paint the wheat field in the distance. I look out the door and paint the man in the hall. I even paint the furniture in my room. The other things in it. But it is not the same.

Q: The same as what?

A: The same as painting outside. I want to do that even at night. There is light at night, too, you know. It is spectacular if you let it enter you. If you dash your eyes around the sky you can see the colors behind the colors of the stars.

Q: And the wind?

A: Sometimes I paint the wind, but my own vision of it. That's what a painter does, you know, he creates reality, he doesn't just copy the reality everyone sees. He sees his own, he makes his own. That's what I try to do. I want to live in my own reality. It must be better than the one I've struggled with my entire life.

Q: Thank you, Vincent.

A: You are very welcome. Shall I call the attendant to let you out?

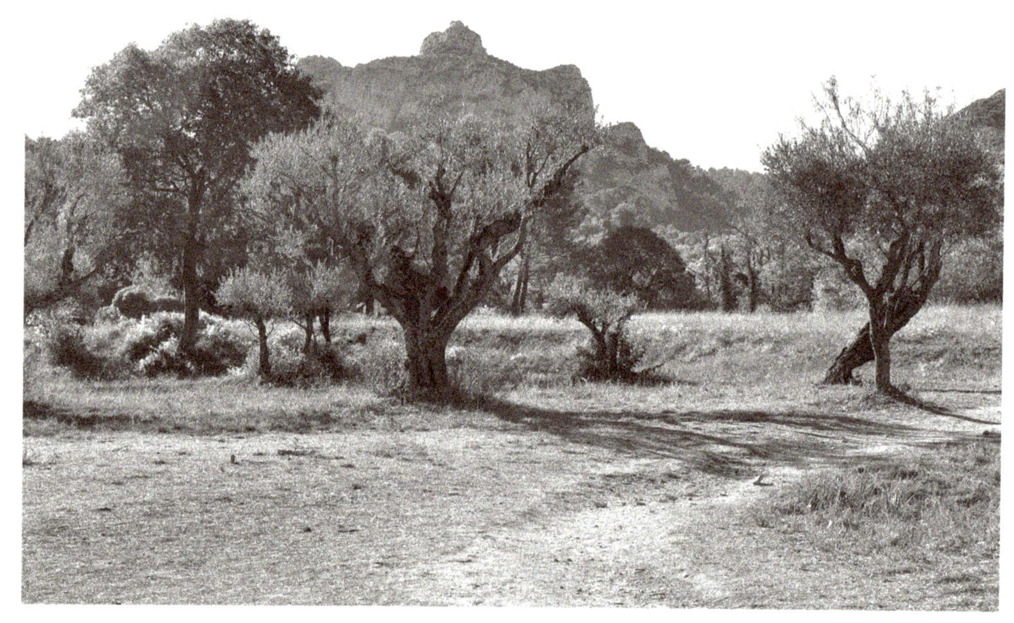

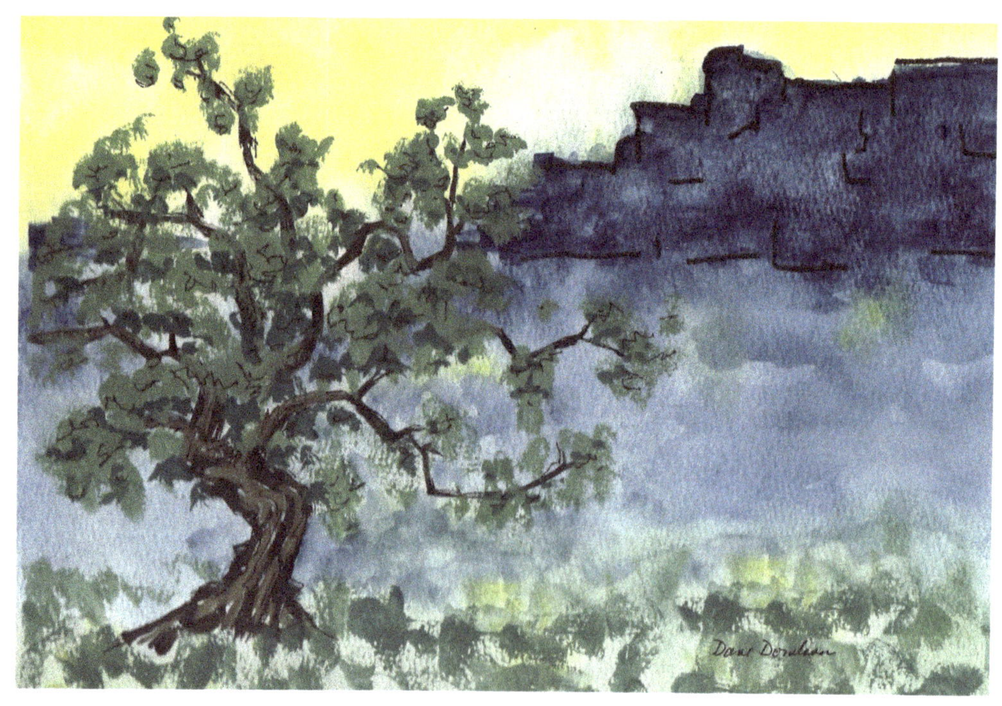
Dave Donelson

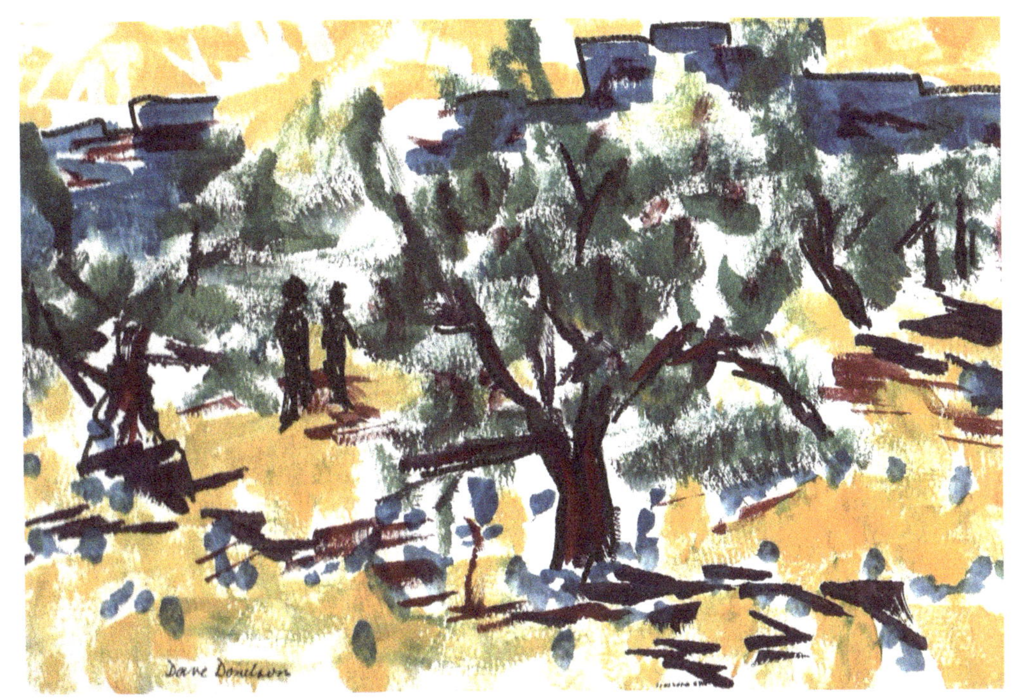

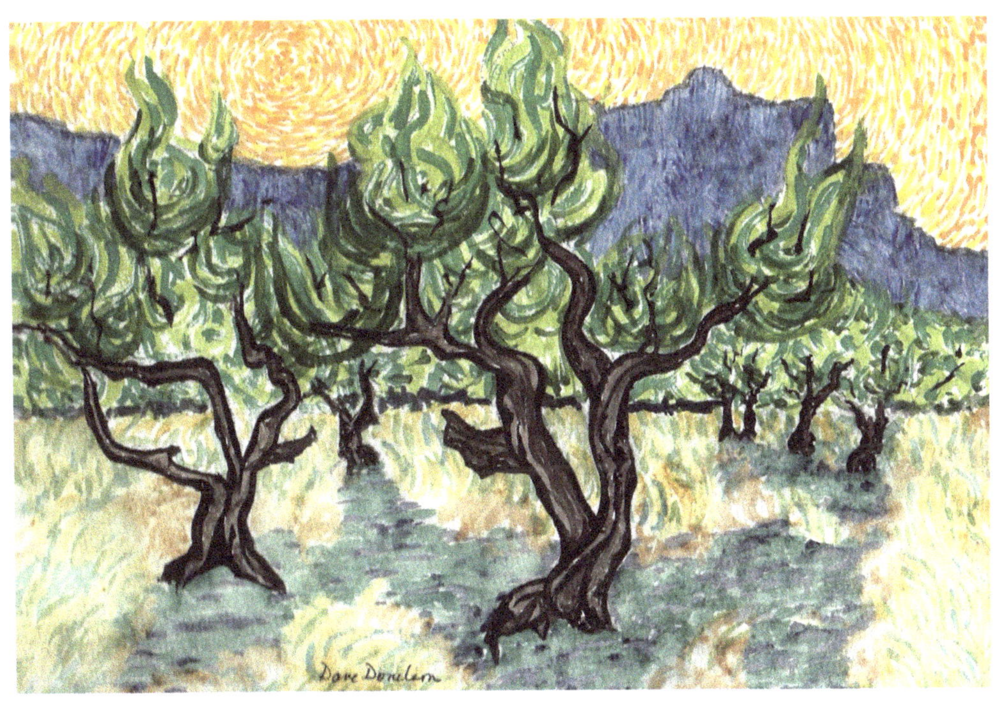

Books by Dave Donelson

Non-fiction

Provence Reflections

Fathers: a Memoir

The Journal of My Seventieth Year
(four volumes)

Poetry

Points in Time

Visions of a Certain Age

Fiction

Hunting Elf

Heart of Diamonds

Blind Curve

Weird Golf

How To

Creative Selling: Boost Your B2B Sales

The Dynamic Manager's Guides
(three volumes)

Slice-Free Golf by Brian Crowell
(editor and photographer)

www.davedonelson.com

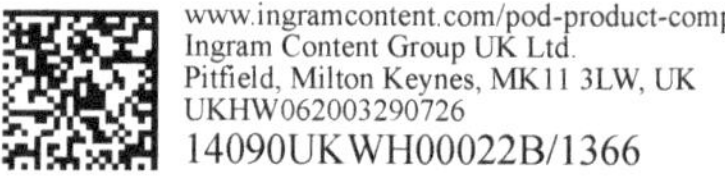
www.ingramcontent.com/pod-product-compliance
Ingram Content Group UK Ltd.
Pitfield, Milton Keynes, MK11 3LW, UK
UKHW062003290726
14090UKWH00022B/1366

9 781963 813036